SECOND EDITION

IN CHARGE 2

An Integrated Skills Course for High-Level Students

Debra Daise

Consulting authors
James E. Purpura
Diane Pinkley

LONGMAN ON THE **WEB**

Longman.com offers online resources for teachers and students. Access our Companion Websites, our online catalog, and our local offices around the world.

Longman English Success offers online courses to give learners flexible study options. Courses cover General English, Business English, and Exam Preparation.

Visit us at **longman.com** and **englishsuccess.com**.

Longman

In Charge 2, Second Edition

Pearson Education, 10 Bank Street, White Plains, NY 10606

Vice president of instructional design: Allen Ascher
Editorial manager: Pam Fishman
Project manager: Margaret Grant
Senior development editor: Eleanor Barnes
Vice president, director of design and production: Rhea Banker
Executive managing editor: Linda Moser
Production manager: Liza Pleva
Production coordinator: Melissa Leyva
Production editor/Reprint manager: Robert Ruvo
Director of manufacturing: Patrice Fraccio
Senior manufacturing buyer: Edie Pullman
Photo research: Aerin Csigay
Cover design: Tracey Cataldo
Text composition: Design 5 Creatives
Text font: 11/14 Palatino
Illustrations: Susan Detrich pp. 3, 7, 20, 28, 29, 33, 49, 87, 90, 112,
    125, 129, 141(bottom); Tim Haggerty pp. 19, 51, 73, 74, 124,
    143, 153; Lou Pappas pg. 96; Phil Scheuer pp. 5, 27, 30, 34,
    43, 65, 67, 68, 83, 84, 137, 140, 141(top), 152; Steve Sullivan pp. 6, 63
Photo credits and text credits: see p. viii

Library of Congress Cataloging-in-Publication Data

Daise, Debra, 1961–
    In charge 2 : an integrated skills course for high-level students / Debra Daise ;
    consulting authors, James E. Purpura, Diane Pinkley.—2nd ed.
        p. cm.
    ISBN 0-13-094260-X
    1. English language—Textbooks for foreign speakers. I. Purpura, James E.
(James Enos), 1951– II. Pinkley, Diane. III. Title

PE1128 .D26 2002
428.2'4—dc21

                                                            2002069488

Printed in the United States of America
1 2 3 4 5 6 7 8 9 10-WC-06 05 04 03 02

CONTENTS

Scope and Sequence iv

Acknowledgments viii

Starting Out 1

UNIT 1 ▪ Buyer Beware 3

UNIT 2 ▪ World of Dreams 15

UNIT 3 ▪ Arms of the Law 27

PROGRESS CHECK ▪ Units 1–3 39

UNIT 4 ▪ Beyond Words 43

UNIT 5 ▪ Amazing Inventions 55

UNIT 6 ▪ Hooked on Horror 67

PROGRESS CHECK ▪ Units 4–6 79

UNIT 7 ▪ A Hard Act to Follow 83

UNIT 8 ▪ The Time of Your Life 95

UNIT 9 ▪ Hot Spots 107

PROGRESS CHECK ▪ Units 7–9 119

UNIT 10 ▪ Far and Wide 123

UNIT 11 ▪ We're All in This Together 135

UNIT 12 ▪ A Laughing Matter 147

PROGRESS CHECK ▪ Units 10–12 159

Pronunciation Symbols 163

Grammar Reference 164

SCOPE AND SEQUENCE

UNIT	Functions	Grammar	Listen	Pronunciation
▪1▪ **Buyer Beware** Page 3	• Asking for advice • Making comparisons • Recommending products • Evaluating products	**Using comparitives, and intensifiers:** • *as/so...as* • *enough* • *very/so/such/too*	A class discussion about advertising ➡ Listening for tone	Understanding rhythm and thought groups; using word stress
▪2▪ **World of Dreams** Page 15	• Describing hypothetical situations • Requesting and giving interpretations • Giving examples • Presenting options	**Transitional expressions:** • *either...or, neither...nor* • *in addition, for example,* etc. • *if, unless,* etc.	Three friends discuss their dreams ➡ Listening for personal interpretation	Using linking and reduction of function words
▪3▪ **Arms of the Law** Page 27	• Asking for and giving or denying confirmation • Giving reasons • Making analogies • Making contrasts	• Tag questions • Participial phrases • Expressing contrast and concession	A student and a professor discuss international law ➡ Listening for analogies	Varying intonation in tag questions

PROGRESS CHECK (Units 1–3) ▪ Page 39

UNIT	Functions	Grammar	Listen	Pronunciation
▪4▪ **Beyond Words** Page 43	• Asking for and giving permission • Asking for and giving clarification • Asking for and giving approval	**Passive modals**	An interview panel discusses job applicants ➡ Listening for expressions of contrast or concession	Perceiving and producing consonant contrasts — minimal pairs
▪5▪ **Amazing Inventions** Page 55	• Describing achievements • Identifying people and objects • Establishing sequences • Giving background information	**Relative clauses:** • with *whose* • with *which* • reduced to phrases	An interview with the biographer of a scientist ➡ Listening for sequence of events and inference	Varying intonation patterns according to sentence type: • statements • information questions • tag questions
▪6▪ **Hooked on Horror** Page 67	• Making/rejecting suggestions • Making alternative suggestions • Talking about causes and effects • Talking about purposes • Retelling narratives	• Causatives: *have, let make, get* • Expressions of cause and effect: *so, since, due to,* etc. • Expressions of purpose: *so that, so as to, in order to,* etc.	A radio interview with a horror writer ➡ Listening for supporting arguments	Using reduction and holding with similar-sounding end and beginning consonants

PROGRESS CHECK (Units 4–6) ▪ Page 79

Speak Out	Read About It	Write About It	Discussion Topics
Discussion ➡ Reviewing discussion skills (1)	"Making Milk Mustache Ads" ➡ Skimming	Writing an Essay ➡ Identifying topic, audience, and purpose	• Aims of advertising • Ethics of advertising • Advertising techniques
Discussion ➡ Reviewing discussion skills (2)	"A Different Field of Dreams" ➡ Previewing	Responding to essay questions ➡ Analyzing essay questions	• Personal significance of dreams • Cultural significance of dreams • Physical aspects of dreaming
Discussion ➡ Reviewing discussion skills (3)	"Informal vs. Formal Traffic Laws" ➡ Categorizing examples	Writing an opinion essay ➡ Deductive and inductive approaches	• The purpose of law • Legal controversies • Spirit vs. letter of the law
Discussion ➡ Reviewing discussion skills (4)	"Space Speaks" ➡ Personaliz-ing information	Writing an exam-style essay ➡ Time management	• Non-verbal messages • Cultural differences in body language • Reading facial expressions • Cultural differences in physical distance
Oral presentations ➡ Components of an oral presentation	"The Pencil" ➡ Distinguishing facts from commentary	Analyzing a research paper ➡ Referring to sources	• Significant inventions and discoveries • Monopolies and innovation • What makes an invention useful
Oral presentations ➡ Introductions and conclusions	"Who Are These Guys?" ➡ Recognizing tone and level of formality	Generating and organizing ideas ➡ Brainstorming, time lines, idea maps, outlines	• People's fascination with horror • Urban legends • Value of horror films, books, etc.

SCOPE AND SEQUENCE

UNIT	Functions	Grammar	Listen	Pronunciation
• 7 • **A Hard Act to Follow** Page 83	• Talking about influences • Assessing abilities • Making recommendations • Expressing necessity	The subjunctive	Two roommates discussing books they are reading ➡ Listening for excerpts and summaries	Recognizing various spellings of the same sound (1)
• 8 • **The Time of Your Life** Page 95	• Talking about preferences • Discussing schedules • Talking about personal characteristics	Gerunds and infinitives	A guest lecturer in a biology class ➡ Taking question-and-answer notes	Recognizing various spellings of the same sound (2)
• 9 • **Hot Spots** Page 107	• Describing objects • Describing processes • Defining terms	**Word order:** • elements of noun phrases • adjectives	A conversation with a vulcanologist ➡ Listening for definitions	Using thought groups to determine sentence stress

PROGRESS CHECK (Units 7–9) ▪ Page 119

UNIT	Functions	Grammar	Listen	Pronunciation
• 10 • **Far and Wide** Page 123	• Making plans • Speculating about the future • Expressing scepticism • Describing people and places • Analyzing experiences	**Future forms:** • future perfect • future perfect progressive **Sentence structure:** • fragments • run-ons	A traveler's description of a foreign haircut ➡ Listening for details	Using stress-timing and linking
• 11 • **We're All in This Together** Page 135	• Complaining • Challenging an argument • Supporting the argument • Persuading others to change	**Irregular nouns:** • subject-verb agreement • countability	A business class discussion on competition and cooperation ➡ Listening for explicit and implicit assumptions	Linking sounds in connected speech: • deletion • addition • change
• 12 • **A Laughing Matter** Page 147	• Telling and explaining jokes • Explaining puns and wordplay • Explaining incongruity • Asking for clarification	**Possessives:** • with *'s* • with *of* Parallel structures	A business seminar on productivity ➡ Listening for supporting details	Shifting sound and stress among members of word families

PROGRESS CHECK (Units 10–12) ▪ Page 159

Speak Out	Read About It	Write About It	Discussion Topics
Oral presentations ➡ Using visual aids	Read About It "The Mistress of Spices" ➡ Reading conversations	Working with sources ➡ Quotation and paraphrase	• Parental influences • Career choices • Life choices
Oral presentations ➡ Delivery tips	"Why Teens Need More Snooze Time" ➡ Reading for credibility	Working with sources ➡ Taking notes and creating a bibliography	• Sleep cycles • Biological rhythms and health • "Day people" vs. "night people"
Oral presentations ➡ Informative talks: Explaining steps of a process	"From the Boundless Deep" ➡ Recognizing literary language	Organizing information ➡ Support paragraphs	• Coping with natural disasters • Mankind's relationship to nature • Science vs. mythology
Discussion ➡ Using and dealing with blocking tactics	"The Enigma of Arrival" ➡ Recognizing descriptive language	Writing an introduction ➡ Considering audience	• Culture shock • Travel as education • Positive and negative effects of tourism
Oral presentations ➡ Giving a persuasive talk	"Get Up a Game" ➡ Evaluating an argument	Writing a conclusion ➡ "Next steps" and memorable closings	• Competitive sports • "I" cultures and "we" cultures • Competition vs. cooperation in business • Cross-cultural humor
Impromptu talks ➡ Preparation and delivery strategies	"Speech Therapy" ➡ Recognizing humor	Completing the research paper ➡ Revising the paper	• The role of incongruity in humor • Physical vs. verbal humor

ACKNOWLEDGMENTS

This book, like other textbooks, could only have been written with the help and support of many people. In particular, I'd like to thank Jim Purpura and Diane Pinkley for their vision, guidance, and suggestions; Marilyn Hochman, Martin Yu, Eleanor Barnes, and Thomas Impola for getting me started, keeping me going, and improving my work; Elizabeth Iannotti, Scott Duarte, Arpad Galaczi, and Evelina Dimitrova for their research; and the teachers, staff, and students at the International English Center who worked with me while I was writing this book. I also must thank Lakhdar Benkobi for his continued love and encouragement, and my housemates, Ambrose and Kilkerra, for not selling all my possessions while I was being inattentive.

Photo credits: p. 3 ©Procter & Gamble; p. 12 Matthew Fox ©1996 National Fluid Milk Processor Promotion Board; p. 13 Mia Hamm ©1999 America's Dairy Farmers and Milk Processors; p. 15 Royalty-Free/Corbis; p. 16 Charles & Josette Lenars/Corbis; p. 17 Catherine Karnow/Corbis; p. 28 Jonathan Nourok/PhotoEdit; p. 36 PhotoDisc/Getty Images; p. 38 Taxi/Getty Images; p. 47 Photofest; p. 55 left: Corbis, right: Oscar White/Corbis; p. 56 top: Reuters NewMedia Inc./Corbis, bottom: ©Tribune Media Services, Inc. All rights reserved. Reprinted with permission; p. 60 Bettmann/Corbis; p. 61 Bettmann/Corbis; p. 71 Photofest; p. 72 Ruggero Vanni/Corbis; p. 75 Blanshard Richard/Corbis Sygma; p. 93 Corbis; p. 94 ©2003 Estate of Pablo Picasso/Artists Rights Society (ARS), New York. Reunion des Musees Nationaux/Art Resource, NY; p. 95 National Geographic/Getty Images; p. 101 Chip Henderson/Index Stock Imagery; p. 104 Rob Lewine Photography/Corbis; p. 107 Ewing Galloway/Index Stock Imagery; p. 108 Douglas Peebles/Corbis; p. 109 AFP/Corbis; p. 113 John Snyder/The Stock Market; p. 117 J. R. Williams/Earth Scenes; p. 118 Roger Ressmeyer/ Corbis; p. 123 Stone/ Getty Images; p. 128 Drawing by Robert Day ©1960, 1988/The New Yorker Magazine, Inc.; p. 131 Dilip Mehta/Contact Press Images/Woodfin Camp & Associates; p. 132 Kunio Owaki/Corbis Stock Market; p. 135 Myrleen Ferguson Cate/PhotoEdit; p. 136 Deborah Davis/PhotoEdit; p. 139 top: Corbis, bottom: Reuters NewMedia Inc./Corbis; p. 144 Wartenberg/ Picture Press/Corbis; p. 149 Bettmann/Corbis; p. 150 Life Magazine Time Warner, Inc.; p. 154 Mary Kate Denny/PhotoEdit.

Text credits: p. 11 from *The Milk Mustache Book* by Jay Schulberg, ©1998 by Jay Schulberg. Photographs and advertisements ©1998 by the National Fluid Milk Processor Promotion Board. Used by permission of Ballantine Books, a division of Random House, Inc.; p. 36 Reprinted from Drivers.com courtesy of PDE Publications; p. 51 from *Silent Language* by Edward T. Hall, ©1959, 1981 by Edward T. Hall. Used by permission of Doubleday, a division of Random House, Inc.; p. 56 This article first appeared in *The Christian Science Monitor* on December 4, 2001 and is reproduced with permission. ©2001 *The Christian Science Monitor* (www.csmonitor.com). All rights reserved; p. 63 Reprinted by special arrangement with the Lyons Press, Guilford, CT; p. 75 ©2002, Chicago Tribune Company. All rights reserved. Used with permission; p. 89 from *The Mistress of Spices* by Chitra Banerjee Divakaruni, ©1997 by Chitra Banerjee Divakaruni. Used by permission of Doubleday, a division of Random House, Inc.; p. 95 Quiz source: *The Body Clock Guide to Better Health* by Michael Smolensky and Lynne Lamberg; p. 103 ©1999 U.S. News & World Report L.P. Reprinted with permission. Also reprinted with the permission of LexisNexis; p. 115 from *Hawaii* by James Michener, ©1959 and renewed 1987 by James A. Michener. Used by permission of Random House, Inc.; p. 131 from *The Enigma of Arrival* by V.S. Naipaul, ©1987 by V.S. Naipaul. Used by permission of Alfred A. Knopf, a division of Random House, Inc.; p. 136 "People Smart: Connecting with Your Social Sense", from *7 Kinds of Smart* by Thomas Armstrong, ©1993 by Thomas Armstrong. Used by permission of Plume, a division of Penguin Putnam Inc.; p. 143 Reprinted with permission of the publisher, from *100 Ways To Motivate Yourself, 2nd ED.* ©2001 by Steve Chandler. Published by Career Press, Franklin Lakes, NJ. All rights reserved; p. 148 from *Relax—You May Only Have A Few Minutes Left* by Loretta LaRoche, ©1998 by Loretta LaRoche. Used by permission of Villard Books, a division of Random House Inc.; p. 155 from *Me Talk Pretty One Day* by David Sedaris. © 2000 by David Sedaris. By permission of Little, Brown and Company, (Inc.).

As you progress in this class, you will have opportunities to learn about the customs, concerns, and goals of people from other cultures. You will also have opportunities to share your own thoughts and experiences with your classmates and teacher. Begin by introducing yourself, finding out about your course, and getting acquainted with your classmates.

Getting Acquainted

1 When you get acquainted with people, you find out information about them. This can sometimes take a long time. Work with a partner. Take turns getting acquainted asking and answering questions on the topics in the box. Take notes.

hometown	hobbies	favorite writer	bad habits
nationality	family	favorite dessert	birthday
car	skills	favorite piece of music	personality
holiday	sports	favorite school subjects	computer

2 Work in small groups. Take turns telling your group members information you learned about your partner in Exercise 1.

3 Setting realistic goals is an important step in achieving success. Think about your goals for this class and complete the chart with your ideas.

SHORT-TERM AND LONG-TERM GOALS

a. Please rate your current English ability in these areas
(0=no ability, 5=excellent ability)

Grammar	0	1	2	3	4	5
Listening	0	1	2	3	4	5
Speaking	0	1	2	3	4	5
Pronunciation	0	1	2	3	4	5
Reading	0	1	2	3	4	5
Writing	0	1	2	3	4	5

b. Realistically, what are your goals for this term?

Grammar	0	1	2	3	4	5
Listening	0	1	2	3	4	5
Speaking	0	1	2	3	4	5
Pronunciation	0	1	2	3	4	5
Reading	0	1	2	3	4	5
Writing	0	1	2	3	4	5

c. What do you think you need to focus on most this term?

d. How do you want to be able to use English in your life?

e. What ability levels do you need to achieve your long-term goal?

Grammar	0	1	2	3	4	5
Listening	0	1	2	3	4	5
Speaking	0	1	2	3	4	5
Pronunciation	0	1	2	3	4	5
Reading	0	1	2	3	4	5
Writing	0	1	2	3	4	5

4 Work in groups. Take turns closing your eyes and placing a finger on one of the spaces in the diagram. Open your eyes, read the question or instruction in the space you chose and carry out the task. Your partners may ask you for clarification or additional information.

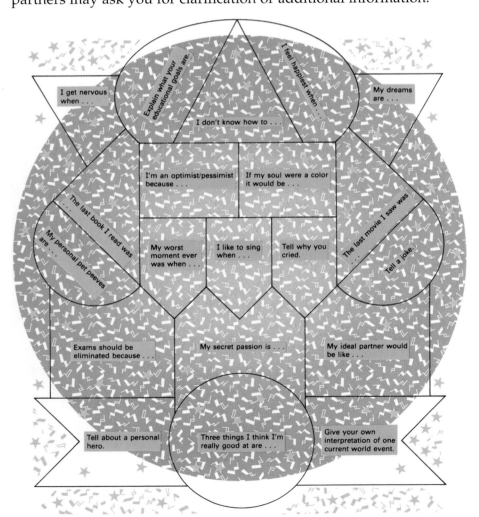

Get out of a jam for less bread.

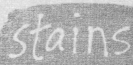

It's a fact. Era costs up to 1/3 less than those pricey brands and helps remove your toughest stains.

The power tool for *stains.*

GETTING STARTED

Warm Up

Most of us see dozens of advertisements a day. We see them in newspapers and magazines, on TV and radio, in the subway, on the sides of buses and buildings, and on the Internet.

1 Work with a partner. Take turns describing an ad that you remember well. Why did it make such an impression on you?

2 Look at the ad above. Who is it designed for? Do you think it is effective? Why? Share your ideas with a partner.

3 Listen to three radio commercials. Decide what each ad is advertising and what group of people each one is designed for. Compare your answers with a partner's.

Figure It Out

Sara Devine and Janet Sawyer are in a recording studio taping a radio advertisement. Read their conversation.

SARA: Hello, everyone. This is Sara Devine. I'm here with my lawyer, Janet Sawyer, to tell you about where to get the best used cars on the market. They're inexpensive, clean, and dependable! They get better gas mileage than any others and will last forever!

5 **JANET:** Sara, can we support those claims? They don't sound very defendable. I have a problem with exaggerating in ads. We'll pay later, you'll see.

SARA: All right, Janet. How's this? Hey, kids, tell your parents to dump your old car. Your friends are making fun of you.

10 It's time to change.

JANET: Sara! You can't use children to sell cars to their parents! It's unethical.

SARA: I'm just trying to advertise my business! That isn't so easy! What do *you* suggest? We can't afford celebrity

15 endorsements or fancy commercials.

JANET: Why don't you just tell the truth? You don't need any gimmicks. You've got great deals here.

SARA: I suppose that's not such a bad idea. How's this? We've got great used cars–immaculate, in top condition, and at great

20 prices. Remember our slogan, "If it doesn't run fine, it's not at Devine."

JANET: That's so much better, see? It wasn't so hard to be honest.

SARA: Can I finish the ad with a lawyer joke? Humor can sell anything, and I know a joke that's funny enough to make

25 even *you* laugh.

JANET: I don't think so. It'd probably be a stereotype and in bad taste. Just say goodbye, Sara.

SARA: Goodbye, Sara.

JANET: Everyone wants to be a comedian. Come see us at Devine Cars.

☑ ④ **Vocabulary Check** Match the words on the left with their meanings on the right.

_____ **1.** claims (line 5)

_____ **2.** unethical (line 12)

_____ **3.** celebrity endorsements (lines 14-15)

_____ **4.** gimmicks (line 17)

_____ **5.** slogan (line 20)

_____ **6.** stereotype (line 26)

_____ **7.** in bad taste (line 26)

a. clever methods of promoting a product

b. photographs of famous people

c. memorable phrase identified with a product, a business, or a politician

d. oversimplified image of a person or group

e. offensive

f. recommendations by famous people

g. unproven statements made as facts

h. immoral or unprincipled

Talk About It

 Two roommates are out shopping. Work with a partner. Take turns being roommates and give recommendations on the products below. Use the conversation as a model.

Example: computers

ROLES	MODEL CONVERSATION	FUNCTIONS
Jeff:	Look at all these computers! I really have to break down and get a new one. Any ideas?	State a wish.
Len:	What's wrong with your old one? Is it too slow?	Ask for details.
Jeff:	Well, it's slow, the monitor is small, and it can't run any of the new games.	Elaborate.
Len:	Why don't you get a DataBorg? My dad swears by his. He got one last month and loves it.	Give a recommendation and a reason for using a product.

Products

a. sports shoes   **c.** PlayStation   **e.** cell phone
b. car   **d.** MP3 player   **f.** (your own idea)

GRAMMAR

Comparisons: *As... As* and *So... As*

We use *as/so... as* to make comparisons between two things that are equal or similar. If the comparison is clear, the second part can be omitted. *As... as* is used to compare adjectives, adverbs, and nouns. To express unequal characteristics, we use the negative form *not as/so... as*.

> This camera is **as expensive as** that camera (is).
>
> It looks **as nice as** that one (does).
>
> It also makes **as little noise** (as yours does).
>
> It's **not so light** (as that one is), and it doesn't take **as clear a picture** (as that one does).
>
> My camera has **as many features as** yours (does), but I didn't spend **as much** (money as you did).

1 Work with a partner. Use the chart to compare the two digital cameras.

Characteristics	DigiPixar	SnapGrabber
a. price	$550	$550
b. weight	6 ounces	8.5 ounces
c. focusing	easy	very easy
d. shutter speed	very fast	fast
e. availability	in many stores	in select stores
f. attachments	many	many

Sufficiency: *Enough*

To indicate that we have a sufficient amount of something, we use *enough +* noun or verb/adjective/adverb + *enough.*

My old laptop isn't **fast enough** for me anymore.

I travel **enough** to need a really reliable computer.

I need one that has **enough** memory for all my files.

I want a good laptop. I don't need to worry about money. I've got **enough** (money).

2 Complete the passages by writing *enough* before or after the word or phrase it describes.

A computer company needed a sales representative to demonstrate their computers to customers in the international market. It put an ad in the newspaper:

The ideal candidate is **(1.)** _____ strong _____enough_____ to lift and carry several computers every day, drives **(2.)** _____ comfortably _____ in traffic to drive on busy streets, speaks **(3.)** _____ Spanish, Japanese, or Arabic _____ to communicate well with customers, and **(4.)** _____ thinks quickly _____ to handle problems.

Soon after that, a man came into the company.

"Just listen," he said to the receptionist. "I'm not (5.) _____ smart_____ to know what I can and can't do, and I don't have (6.) _____ patience _____ to make an appointment. I'm here about that ad in the paper. I don't have (7.) _____ strength _____ to lift a computer monitor, and I don't see (8.)_____ well _____ to drive in traffic. I don't (9.) _____ know _____ to say "hello" in any other language.

"So what are you here for?" said the receptionist.

"Well," said the man, "I just wanted you to know that I'm not (10.) _____ qualified _____ to sell your computers."

Intensifers: *Very, So, Such,* and *Too*

Intensifiers such as *very, so,* and *too*, make adjectives, adverbs, and nouns phrases stronger. They express either a positive or a negative meaning and appear before adjectives and adverbs. *Such* is used to modify a noun phrase. *So* means to a large degree. *Too* expresses a sense of excess.

> That computer is **very** expensive. In fact, it's **so** expensive, I'll never pay for it.
> You have **such** an expensive computer. It's **too** expensive for me.

3 Look at the ad. Then read the critique. Check the features that are OK. Compare your answers with a partner's.

DEVINE CARS

New cars! Used cars with warranties! Nobody beats our selection and prices! Our cars are Devine!

CRITIQUE

The basic design of the ad is very nice. The print is too small, and the letters look so hard to read. The people aren't too bad, but there are too many cars. The business name stands out very clearly.

Features

☐ **a.** basic design
☐ **b.** colors
☐ **c.** print size

☐ **d.** letters
☐ **e.** people
☐ **f.** number of cars

☐ **g.** business name
☐ **h.** credibility
☐ **i.** (your own idea)

Negative Intensifiers

We use *not so/not as* to express an unequal comparison. We use these to sound less blunt or direct.

> My camera isn't working **as well as** it should work. = My camera is**n't** working **so well**.
>
> I don't have **as big a camera as** many others do. = I don't have **such a big camera**.

  4 **Check Your Understanding** On a separate sheet of paper, shorten the underlined phrases using *so* and *such*. Make any necessary changes.

a. An advertisement needs to convince people to buy a product. If no one buys the product, the ad isn't <u>as successful as it should be</u>.

b. An ad doesn't need to attract <u>as many people as you might think</u>.

c. Usually, an advertising agency targets a specific group of people and doesn't worry <u>as much as it could about the rest of the people</u>.

d. For example, an advertising agency knows that teenagers aren't <u>as likely as other people are to worry about life insurance</u>.

e. Television isn't always <u>as effective a medium as people think it is</u>.

f. It isn't <u>as good a channel as other media are to sell products that need detailed explanations</u>.

  5 **Express Yourself** Choose an ad you like from a magazine. Discuss the strong and weak points of the ad with a partner. Who does it target? Compare your reactions with your partner's.

LISTENING and SPEAKING

Listen: An Advertising Class

 1 **Before You Listen** Is the purpose of advertising to inform consumers about a product or service or to persuade consumers to buy something? Discuss your answers with a partner.

 Listening for Tone When listening for personal interpretation, effective listeners pay attention to the speaker's tone of voice in order to understand the speaker's feeling about what is being said. In conversation, listening for the tone helps the listener understand more than what is actually stated in words.

🎧 **2** Listen to a class discussion about advertising and take notes. As you listen, circle the answer that best completes each sentence and support each with examples.

1. The overall tone of the discussion was _____.
   a. humorous   **b.** serious   **c.** complaining

2. When the professor asked Erica a question, her response was _____.
   a. dismissing   **b.** sarcastic   **c.** thoughtful

3. When Courtney talked about creativity in advertising, she sounded _____.
   a. disappointed   **b.** enthusiastic   **c.** suspicious

3 Listen again and answer the questions with a partner.
   a. What are the two main purposes of advertising?
   b. What are four important things to consider when designing an ad?
   c. Which of the following techniques do you think advertisers avoid? Explain.

   - stereotyping
   - talking about competitors
   - using offensive words
   - paying a celebrity to sell the product
   - exaggerating

Pronunciation

Rhythm and Thought Groups

Every word consists of at least one stressed syllable. Stressed syllables are pronounced louder and held longer than unstressed syllables. Pitch changes too. When several words form a complete idea, they create a thought group with a chain of stressed and unstressed syllables. This chain has an uneven, yet distinct rhythm in English.

4 Identify the thought groups with a slash (/). Predict which syllables are stressed in each thought group and underline them.

> But when I got to the supermarket, I couldn't believe my eyes! They were having the most incredible bake sale that I'd ever seen! Everything was piping hot and half off. And they were giving people samples of the sweets! So I tried everything they had and spent all my money. When I got home, my wife told me I'd forgotten the milk. Oh, well!

🎧 **5** Listen to the paragraph to check your predictions.

6 Work with a partner. Take turns saying the sentences.

Speak Out

 Reviewing Discussion Skills (1) All of us participate in meetings and discussions at work or school. An effective discussion, whether in an academic or business setting, requires management. Three important aspects of discussion management include introducing the discussion, organizing the discussion, and moving the discussion forward.

Introducing a Discussion
- greeting the participants
- introducing new participants
- stating the purpose of the discussion
- presenting and agreeing on an agenda
- introducing the topic for discussion

Organizing a Discussion
- listing the main points for discussion
- establishing their priority of importance
- establishing the time available

Moving a Discussion Forward
- acknowledging the last speaker's contribution
- asking for brief comments before going on
- stating the next point of discussion

---

7 Decide if these expressions are **I** (introducing a discussion), **O** (organizing a discussion), or **M** (moving a discussion forward).

_____ **a.** Ms. Mahootian is our new consultant.

_____ **b.** We'll focus on outlining the steps to . . . .

_____ **c.** Any comments before we move on to the next item on the agenda?

_____ **d.** Dr. Jacobs, would you please begin our discussion?

_____ **e.** Our last fifteen minutes will be devoted to . . . .

_____ **f.** Good morning, and thanks for coming at such an early hour.

_____ **g.** Our most important task today is . . . .

_____ **h.** Your comments are appreciated, Jeff, but we have to go on to . . . .

_____ **i.** The next item under consideration is the budget.

_____ **j.** We have half an hour to pick the new commercial.

8 Work in small groups. Take turns using the topics to introduce, organize, and move a discussion forward, as needed.

Discussion Topics
a. an ad aimed at teenagers
b. an environmental protection campaign
c. a protest about a TV commercial
d. a survey to determine consumer habits
e. two political advertisements
f. (your own idea)

Read About It

 Before You Read Answer the following questions with a partner.
   a. Have you seen ads for milk before? What did they look like?
   b. Look at the title of the reading selection. What do you think it is about?

STRATEGY ▶ **Skimming** Efficient readers quickly skim the key ideas of a passage before reading it. Because the key ideas often appear in the section headings, readers quickly discover the key ideas by skimming the headings. Once they are aware of the main ideas, they are better prepared to recognize the important details of the passage.

2 Skim the headings. As you read, note the key ideas.

3 Now read the entire selection.

Making Milk Mustache Ads
by Jay Schulberg

In the 1990s, the American milk industry wanted to let the public know that people were drinking less milk and, as a result, were suffering more health problems, such as weak bones and fractured hips. The milk industry and the American government challenged Bozell Worldwide, an advertising agency, to
5   design a campaign to educate Americans on the benefits of drinking milk. In The Milk Mustache Book, creative director Jay Schulberg wrote about how the ad campaign got started.

Milk. What a surprise!

We accepted the challenge. Lots of research was done. We learned why many
10   people stopped drinking milk or were drinking less.

But how could we get them to reconsider?

Fundamentally, it all came down to common sense. Don't tell me milk's good for me—my mother tried that one. Tell me something new and change my mind; make me look at milk in a new way. We knew that if we told you
15   milk is good for you, most likely you would say, "Thank you very much, go away." Or if we told you milk builds strong bones, you might respond with a tinge of sarcasm, "No kidding." Then mutter, "Go away." We had to tell people something new and meaningful, something they did not already know.

So we dug up some facts. Most people believed that when fat is taken out
20   of milk, all the vitamins and minerals go, too. Absolutely not true. Fat-free and low-fat milk have all the calcium, vitamins and minerals as whole milk. Another fact: women need the calcium in milk for constant bone mass replenishment. If they don't get it, they risk bone density loss, fractured bones, or osteoporosis later....

(continued on next page)

A face that makes you smile

The next question was: how do we create an educational campaign? Informational campaigns tend to be boring and lecturing—ours had to be simple, arresting, charming, and fun.

We deliberately designed it as a poster campaign. We wanted a strong, surprising visual that would stop someone cold in a magazine. Think about it. Most magazines are crammed with editorial matter and cluttered with ads. Everyone is fighting for your attention. A poster with an unexpected face staring right back at you, especially if it were a face that made you smile or laugh, would probably stop you from turning the page.

Next we limited the copy to only four lines. The opening and closing lines would reflect the personality of the person shown. Tucked between the opening and closing lines would be a surprising nugget of new information about milk. We believed that if the visual had stopping power and if the copy was charmingly and engagingly written, if it made you smile, we had a very good chance of getting our health message across. It reflects a fundamental truth about human nature: people are more likely to accept what you say if you present it in an engaging fashion rather than if you lecture them.

Democracy is over. This is what we're going to do!

[Schulberg assembled teams to work on the campaign. As a creative director, he preferred to let the teams make their own decisions rather than telling them what to do.]

Just before I left for Cannes [for the annual International Advertising Festival], I asked the teams of writers and art directors to show me where they were in the development of ideas. I would have very little time after my return before I was scheduled to show our recommended campaign to our client.

I was taken aback when the teams showed me their ideas. We had an upside-down cow. Why? I don't know except its creator thought it was cool. We had the word "milk" embossed on the side of the page. Do you know anyone who reads a page sideways? Better yet, do you know anyone who reads a page sideways looking for embossed letters? We were not off to an auspicious start. There was a milk mustache on some character, but it did not jump out at me. I told the teams they should continue working, and I would review their work in a week's time when I returned. The only thing I thought might have promise was the milk mustache, but I thought that it had to be executed in an entirely different way. "Could we continue working on our other stuff, too?" one team member asked, meaning the upside-down cow and embossed lettering. "Sure," I replied, "but spend the bulk of your time on new ideas or the milk mustache."

Great clients make great advertising

[By the time he returned, the teams still hadn't created an ad that Schulberg liked, so he got two of his best people to work on the mustache campaign. The milk industry's representative, Charlie Decker, liked it but asked them to use celebrities rather than ordinary people.]

I have to admit I wasn't too keen on the use of celebrities; I always thought it was the last refuge of tired brains. That probably was because celebrities had been overused in advertising in the preceding two decades.... Celebrities are only effective if they are believable spokespeople
75 for the product or the brand. However, Charlie asked, so we would try it.

[Schulberg then assigned the copywriter the task of writing the copy.]

Is using a milk mustache a new idea? No. Is using a
80 celebrity a new idea? No. Is using a celebrity with a milk mustache a new idea? Yes! A very big idea, as it turns out.

4 Work with a partner and answer the questions.

a. Why did the advertising agency need to do research on milk?

b. What decisions did they make about their campaign?

c. Why did the ad team use a poster campaign?

d. Why did they use celebrities?

e. What was the result of the ad campaign? How do you know?

f. What is the tone of this article? Relaxed? Scientific? Sarcastic?

 5 **Vocabulary Check** Decide if the terms below are **A** (advertising terms) or **M** (medical terms). Compare your answers with a partner's. What context clues helped you?

_____ **1.** fractured (line 3)

_____ **2.** bone mass replenishment (lines 22-23)

_____ **3.** bone density loss (line 23)

_____ **4.** osteoporosis (line 24)

_____ **5.** visual (line 30)

_____ **6.** editorial matter (line 31)

_____ **7.** copy (line 36)

_____ **8.** embossed (line 55)

Think About It

6 According to *The Milk Mustache Book*, the target audience for the milk ads was women. What information about milk would *you* have included in the ads for women? Which celebrities would you have used? Explain.

Write: Topic, Audience, and Purpose

STRATEGY A clear sense of topic, audience, and purpose is important to writers in planning, drafting, and revising any piece of writing. Efficient writers review a work in progress frequently to make sure that it is consistent with their original aims.

The writer must first consider the scope of the intended topic. It is important that the scale of the topic is appropriate for the piece. The topic should be neither too broad nor too narrow. Equally important is the audience. The writer should use language that is appropriate for the intended audience and should know something about their tastes, opinions, and knowledge of the topic. Finally, an effective writer maintains a clear purpose. A piece of writing may have multiple purposes, for example, "to entertain while persuading." However, there should be one purpose that maintains focus and gives the piece a consistent tone.

 Read the sample essay openings and decide what the topic is, who the intended audience is, and what the main purpose of the text would be. On what did you base your decisions? Discuss your answers with a partner.

1. When we consider the prevalence of product placement in Hollywood movies, we can see that, although the moviegoer spends good money to escape constant and obnoxious commercial interruptions, there really is no refuge anywhere from the tyranny of the marketplace. What, if anything, can be done? The curse of these "stealth ads" goes back to the Silent Era, when…

   TOPIC: _____ AUDIENCE: _____ PURPOSE: _____

2. Advertising has been a part of the human experience since the first stirrings of commerce in the dawn of civilization. However, a real quantum leap in the power of advertising occurred with the rise of electronic media. If we trace the explosive growth of the advertising industry from the early days of radio through the era of the Internet and cable television, it is clear that…

   TOPIC: _____ AUDIENCE: _____ PURPOSE: _____

Write About It

 Choose one of the topics. Decide on an audience and purpose and write an essay.

> - advertising and the economy
> - the best ad I've ever seen
> - Internet advertising
> - political ads
> - prohibitions in advertising
> - ads and humor
> - offensive commercials
> - (your own idea)

  Check Your Writing Exchange papers with a partner. Use the questions below to give feedback to your partner. When you get your paper back, revise as necessary.

> - Is the scope of the topic appropriate to a paper of this length? If not, does the topic need to be narrowed or broadened?
> - Are the content and language appropriate for the intended audience?
> - Is the purpose clear? Does the paper maintain its focus, without digression?

GETTING STARTED

Warm Up

We all dream, whether we remember or not. For centuries people have tried to interpret what their dreams have meant. Are dreams messages sent from our unconscious, predictions of the future, or the brain's way of cleaning out information?

1 Look at the list of dream images below. What might they represent? Share your ideas with the class.

| a road | the sky | snow | a garden | an open door | a light | sand |

2 Listen to an account of a dream. Circle the items below that are mentioned. Compare your answers with a partner's.

| sand | a storm | scorpions | snakes | the sun | sisters | sickness | snow |

3 Now listen to an interpretation of the dream. Find an image from the dream that represents each concept, and write it on the line. Do you agree with the interpretation?

Concept	Image		Concept	Image
a. safety	_____		**c.** an enemy	_____
b. few resources	_____		**d.** trust	_____

Figure It Out

4 Dreams in the past were considered messages. Read how the ancient Egyptians and Greeks viewed dreams.

It is difficult to compare the dreams of modern people with those of the ancients, for the ancients neither recorded the dreams of common people, nor considered them important. The dreams of kings, queens, pharaohs, and other leaders, however, were seen as messages from the gods, just as these leaders were often seen as offspring
5 of the gods. Furthermore, when a dream was proven to be prophetic, it reinforced this religious belief and gave the leader more incentive to record the prophecy.

Pharaoh Thutmes IV, for example, had a stone tablet put up in front of the Great Sphinx of Giza in Egypt to commemorate a dream that he had had
10 before becoming pharaoh. Prince Thutmes lay down to rest in the shade of the monument at midday and dreamed that the Sphinx spoke to him, telling him that he would be pharaoh—as long as he would promise to clear away the sand that had begun to cover the
15 Sphinx. The Prince agreed, and, when he removed the sand from around the monument, he became pharaoh.

A modern interpretation might conclude either that the dream was coincidental or that the Pharaoh "remembered" his dream when history showed it to be true. Neither version would be acceptable to one who believed in divine visions manifested in dreams.

20 Additional examples of such beliefs lie in numerous plaques found in ancient Greek temples, especially temples of Asclepius. These plaques tell of illnesses diagnosed and remedied through dreams. The afflicted would be brought to the temple and told to await a message from the gods that would come in a dream and instruct the person on how to cure the illness. The number of plaques suggests success in this form of treatment,
25 though the exact mechanism of success could well be disputed by modern physicians.

 5 **Vocabulary Check** Work with a partner. Use the context of the reading to discuss possible meanings of the following words.

a. offspring (line 4) **c.** shade (line 11) **e.** remedied (line 22)
b. prophetic (line 5) **d.** coincidental (line 17) **f.** afflicted (line 22)

Talk About It

6 Two friends are discussing their dreams. Work with a partner. Take turns being the dreamer and the friend, and discuss what the images on the next page might represent in dreams. Use the conversation as a model.

Example: flying

ROLES	MODEL CONVERSATION	FUNCTIONS
Dreamer:	I had the best dream last night. I dreamed I could fly, just like Superman.	Describe a dream.
Curious Friend:	Wow! Any idea what it could mean?	Request an interpretation.
Dreamer:	Well, it must be a good sign. Either I'm going on a trip, or I'm turning into a butterfly.	Give two possible interpretations.

<u>Dream Images</u>

a. fire   **c.** darkness   **e.** speaking with a dead relative

b. falling   **d.** being chased   **f.** (your own idea)

GRAMMAR

Either...Or and Neither...Nor

We use *either...or* to show that one of two options is possible, and *neither...nor* to show that both options are impossible. When using *either...or* and *neither...nor*, we must use parallel grammatical structures (*either* + noun; *or* + noun/ *either* + verb phrase; *or* + verb phrase), and the verb must agree with the subject that is closest to it in the sentence.

> **Either** my nieces **or** my nephew writes every dream down.
>
> She **neither** sees color **nor** hears music in her dreams.

 On a separate sheet of paper, combine the following sentences, using *either...or* or *neither...nor*. Do not change the meaning of the sentences.

a. The Lakota people of North America believe that dreams can carry positive forces. They also believe that dreams can carry negative forces.

b. The Lakota put a dream catcher on the wall to catch evil dreams and negative forces. Sometimes they put the dream catcher above the bed.

Dream Catcher

c. Good dreams are not caught in the dream catcher. Positive forces are not caught in the dream catcher.

d. In the morning, the sun sometimes makes the evil dreams fall through the hole in the middle of the web. Sometimes the sun makes the evil dreams slide down the feathers or leather strings at the bottom.

e. The negative forces do not remain with the dreamer. They do not influence the dreamer.

2 Find the mistake in each sentence and correct it.

Example: People in the West think that dreams either ~~is~~ *are* internal messages or have no meaning.

   a. A person in the Rarámuri culture who claims to visit faraway places in dreams is considered neither crazy or dishonest.

   b. Either information about other people or warnings about the future is often the subject of the dreams.

   c. A dream may be interpreted by either the dreamer himself nor an older member of the family.

   d. The whole community honors the people who can either cure others through their dreams or predicting the future.

Transitional Devices

We use transitional devices to link ideas across clauses and sentences. They let us know that there is a logical connection and what kind of connection it is. Transitional devices can be used to signal additional information, hypothetical situations, or examples.

Additional information
(and, also, in addition (to), additionally, besides, moreover, furthermore)

I fell asleep **and** dreamed about our travels.
I see a lot of action in my dreams **in addition to** bright colors.
I write down my dreams **besides** telling them to my friends.
I like to dream; **furthermore**, I dream often.

Hypothetical Situations
(as long as, in case of, in the event [of/that] if, or [else], otherwise, unless)

I have to write down my dreams, **or else** I won't be able to remember them.
I try to get enough sleep; **otherwise**, my dreams are unpleasant.
Unless I have a light on, I have bad dreams.

Giving Examples
(for example, for instance, like)

Some people, **like** me, hear music in their dreams.

Some transitional devices (*and, but, nor, or, yet*) join two independent or main clauses. Others (*although, because, if, when*) connect an independent clause with a dependent clause. Still others (*however, furthermore, therefore*) join two independent clauses or sentences.

3 Look at the examples in the box above. What is the punctuation for each type of transitional device?

4 Circle the transitional device that best completes each sentence. Indicate the punctuation. Then work with a partner. Compare your answers and explain your choices.

A cultural anthropologist wanted to learn about the Cree people of Canada. **(1. Besides/Or else)** learning about the Cree's beliefs in dreams, she learned about her own beliefs. She found that the Cree believe that a dead person may bring messages in a dream from the world of the dead. The dreamer is required to act on these messages; **(2. such as/otherwise)**, he or she might be punished for ignoring them. **(3. In the event of/ In addition to)** bad news, the dreamer may be reluctant to act on the communication. One time, a woman dreamed that her dead cousin sent her some messages. The woman didn't want to give anyone bad news, but **(4. unless/like)** she delivered the messages, her dead ancestors would be angry. Soon after the dream, the woman lost her voice. She believed she had to deliver the messages, **(5. in addition/or else)** she wouldn't be able to talk again. Perhaps **(6. if/unless)** her cousin comes to her dreams again, she might obey her more quickly. **(7. As long as/Otherwise)**, she might lose her voice again.

For the Cree, the power of a dream doesn't come from the dream itself but from the forces behind the dream. The woman who lost her voice, **(8. such as/for example)**, wanted to ignore the dream, but she acted because of her duty to her relatives. Understanding the culture of the dreamer, **(9. in addition to/in the event that)** beliefs about the origin of dreams, is an important factor in understanding the power of dreams.

5 Complete the joke by writing the correct words from the box.

or	for example	in addition to	in the event that
such as	furthermore	unless	otherwise

"Doctor," said the woman, "every night my son dreams he's a chicken, and then he starts acting like one. **(1.)** _____, he flaps his arms like wings, puts his head down to the ground, and starts eating bugs. **(2.)** _____, his head goes back and forth when he walks, and, **(3.)** _____ he's still dreaming at dawn, he comes into my room and wakes me up."

"This is very serious," said the doctor. "You should bring him to me at once. **(4.)** _____, he might develop other strange behaviors, **(5.)** _____ building a nest, **(6.)** _____ the things you've already told me."

"OK, Doctor," said the woman. "But I'm going to miss the fresh eggs."

6 **Check Your Understanding** Complete the sentences using the words in parentheses and your own information.

1. I believe dreams serve a purpose (**because**) _____ .
2. Dreams can seem real, (**however**) _____ .
3. Some dreams are crazy; (**for example**) _____ .
4. I usually fall asleep quickly (**unless**) _____ .
5. I sleep soundly (**as long as**) _____ .

 7 **Express Yourself** Write a paragraph describing and interpreting a vivid dream. Be sure to use transition words appropriately. Then read your paragraph to a partner.

LISTENING and SPEAKING

Listen: What's in a Dream?

1 **Before You Listen** Some people say that dreaming about losing money means that you will receive it. Have you ever heard this? What other sayings about dreams do you know? Share your information with a partner.

STRATEGY **Interpreting a Personal Narrative** A personal narrative is often open to interpretation. When listening for personal interpretation, it is important to identify the speaker's feelings and attitudes toward the experience and to use this information to understand the narrative.

2 Listen to three friends talk about their dreams. As you listen, identify each speaker's feelings and attitudes toward dreams, and fill in the chart. Then compare your answers with a partner's.

	Dream	Attitude Toward Dream
Keiko		
Bianca		
Antonio		

3 Listen again. Then work in small groups and discuss the questions below.

  a. Why do you think Keiko had her dream? What could she learn from it?

  b. Do you think Antonio will change his opinion of dreams after the conversation? Why or why not?

  c. Do you believe that dreams can predict the future? Why or why not?

  d. Have you had a "dream" experience similar to one of the speaker's in the conversation? What lesson did you learn from it?

Pronunciation

> ### Linking and Reductions
> When we speak, all the words in a single thought are joined together. The function words are often reduced and linked. However, when we emphasize a point, we use the full forms.
>
> **A:** *Where is he now?*   becomes   ˌhwɛriˈnau
> **B:** *He's at the gym.*   becomes   ˌhizætðəˈjɪm

4 Work with a partner. Practice saying both forms of the words below.

Full Form	Linked and Reduced Form
bread and butter	bredn'bʌtɚ
cup of coffee	kʌpə'kɔfi
used to go	yustə'gou
going to go	gʌnə'gou
has to go	hæstə'gou
could have gone	kudə'gɔn

5 Predict which words will be linked and reduced in the conversation and circle them.

  A: When I was young, I used to dream I was being chased by tornados.
  B: Really? What do you think that's supposed to mean?
  A: I must have had a lot stress then.
  B: You've got to be kidding! What could have been so stressful?
  A: Being chased by all those tornados every night.

 6 Listen to the conversation to check your predictions.

7 Work with a partner. Read the conversation above, focusing on the linked and reduced forms.

Speak Out

Reviewing Discussion Skills (2) Once the discussion has been introduced, participants need to make sure that all group members take turns, stay on track, and clarify misunderstandings.

Taking Turns

Jane, we still haven't heard your opinion.

Jesse, you have the floor.

Staying on Track

Sorry to cut your story short, Bill, but we need to finish.

If we could all get back to the topic at hand . . .

Clarifying Miscommunications

Let me rephrase what I think you said.

What I meant to say was . . .

---

8 Decide if these expressions are **T** (turn taking), **S** (staying on track), or **C** (clarifying miscommunication).

_____ **a.** If I understand you correctly, you're saying that . . .

_____ **b.** And now let's hear from . . .

_____ **c.** I think I missed something in our conversation here.

_____ **d.** The jokes will have to wait for the break, George.

_____ **e.** Perhaps Doctor McCormack has something to add.

_____ **f.** Are you telling us that . . . ?

_____ **g.** Could we stick to the main point?

_____ **h.** Can we stop and recap? I'm a little confused.

9 Work in small groups. Take turns discussing the topics. Use language appropriate for taking turns, staying on track, and clarifying miscommunications, as needed.

> * comparing personal dreaming patterns
> * debating the possibility of learning while asleep
> * contrasting cultural differences in dream interpretations
> * planning an art exhibit that portrays dreams
> * (your own idea)

Read About It

1 **Before You Read** How do you usually feel when you wake up? How do you feel when someone wakes you up suddenly? Share your responses with a partner.

STRATEGY **Previewing** When reading for understanding, effective readers often preview the material they will be reading in order to focus on the topic. One way of previewing a passage is to read the first sentence of each paragraph to get an overview of the points that will be covered.

2 Read the first sentence in each paragraph. What will the passage be about?

3 Read the passage. As you read, use the preview information to help you focus on key ideas and examples.

A Different Field of Dreams

You are walking into a dormitory in New York City, preparing to start studying at a college. Your bed is in a computer lab, and every night you have to ask people to leave so that you can get some sleep. You are very tired, but nobody will leave. You wake up suddenly and realize that you are neither in a college nor in a computer lab.
5   You've been dreaming.

Why do we dream? How do we dream? Sleep researchers may not have exact answers to these questions, but they have found that dreaming has some interesting physiological effects.

When we sleep, our bodies change, especially our brains and nervous systems. Our
10 muscles relax, and the levels of chemicals around our brains change, either increasing or decreasing from their usual amounts. These changes, in effect, give us different brains when we sleep by allowing different areas to be more, or less, active. The front area of the brain, which is responsible for making logical connections, is inactive, while the areas of the brain associated with emotion are much more active
15 than usual. Because the logic areas are not active, situations that seem to be illogical while we are awake are accepted during sleep. In this way, we may have fantastic dreams of places and situations that we would probably never encounter during our waking lives.

Some people claim that we can solve problems through dreaming by taking
20 advantage of these illogical dreams. By making and accepting connections that our logical minds would otherwise reject, we sometimes come up with creative solutions to difficult problems.

(continued on next page)

We begin to dream a few minutes after we fall asleep. We first have a short period of quiet sleep, which deepens as our muscles relax. We cycle through periods of quiet sleep and rapid-eye-movement (REM) sleep. During REM sleep, the muscles below our necks are paralyzed, but our eyes, as the name indicates, are very active. During this type of sleep, our bodies do not respond as easily to external forces, such as light or sound, but the brain and nervous system are quite active. The dreams that we have while in REM sleep are much more vivid and active than those of quiet sleep.

Researchers have found that learning may be affected by REM sleep and by the quiet sleep we get early in the cycle. We seem to need at least six hours of sleep every day in order to remember a new task well. In the event that a sleeper is awakened during critical periods of sleep, such as early quiet sleep or late REM sleep, he or she will not do well on later tests of learning. Another sleeper who is awakened the same number of times, but not during critical sleep periods, will do better. Researchers suggest that the interaction between different types of sleep may help us assimilate new knowledge or skills.

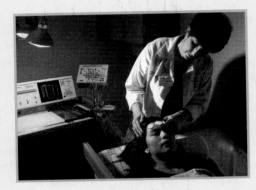

Furthermore, researchers have found that moods are affected by dreaming. If people are unhappy when they go to sleep, they usually wake up in a better mood if they are allowed to go through a full cycle of dreams. This happens because the dreams at the beginning of the sleep cycle are usually more negative than those at the end. That is, the most positive dreams are the ones that the dreamer has just before waking up. In contrast, when depressed people are unhappy before going to sleep, they usually have increasingly negative dreams throughout the sleep cycle, thereby waking up more depressed than when they went to sleep.

Some people suffering from depression, however, do have more positive dreams at the end of the sleep cycle. These are the people who will probably come out of their depression. Although researchers may not know exactly what the relationship is between sleep and depression, it is hoped that people suffering from depression can learn to affect their dreams so that the dreams end more positively. By doing so, they may be able to lessen, or even end, their depression.

Dreams have been fascinating us for thousands of years, and for thousands of years we have been trying to understand them and their relationship to our waking lives. We have found out much, but chances are, we still have a lot to learn in the years to come.

Answer the questions. Compare your answers with a partner's.

   a. Why do we accept situations in dreams that we wouldn't accept in our waking lives?

   b. What does REM stand for, and what are two differences between REM sleep and quiet sleep?

   c. The reading mentions three possible benefits of dreaming. What are they?

   d. How do depressed and non-depressed people differ in their dreaming?

 Vocabulary Check Work with a partner. Use the context of the reading on pages 23–24 to discuss possible meanings of the following words.

   a. physiological (line 8)   **e.** critical (lines 34, 38)

   b. illogical (lines 15, 20)   **f.** assimilate (line 41)

   c. claim (line 19)   **g.** thereby (line 51)

   d. nervous (line 28)

Think About It

Work with a partner and discuss the questions.

- Do you usually remember your dreams? Describe some of them.
- Do your dreams ever affect your moods? Explain.
- Do you believe dreams can predict the future?

Write: Responding to Essay Questions

 Essays written in test situations present special challenges. In most writing situations, the writer decides on the topic, audience, and purpose. However, in an essay test, the topic is given in the question; the audience is assumed to be the teacher or the person who will grade the test; the purpose may range from a summary to persuasion or argumentation. Below is a list of common essay types you might be familiar with.

   a. cause and effect   **e.** description of a process

   b. comparison and contrast   **f.** argumentation

   c. definition   **g.** summary

   d. exemplification

7 Which essay type is most appropriate for each writing task below? Write the letter from the list on page 25 on the line.

_____ **1.** analyzing and discussing the good and bad points of the topic

_____ **2.** discussing the reasons for something and the related results and consequences

_____ **3.** describing how to do something or how something works

_____ **4.** discussing the similarities and differences between two or more things

_____ **5.** stating the most important ideas, issues, points, or steps of the topic in a relatively short form

_____ **6.** identifying what something is and what makes it different from other similar things in its class

_____ **7.** giving examples of a theme or important idea

8 Read the essay questions below. What type of essay would be appropriate? Write the letter from the list on page 25 on the line. Then discuss your answers with a partner.

_____ **1.** How are dreams interpreted in the Rarámuri culture?

_____ **2.** What is a dream?

_____ **3.** What causes our dreams?

_____ **4.** How effective is using dreams to predict the future?

_____ **5.** Give examples of cultures that use dreams in religious ceremonies.

_____ **6.** Compare the Rarámuri's use of dreams with the Cree's.

_____ **7.** Briefly state the main points of the lecture on dream interpretation.

Write About It

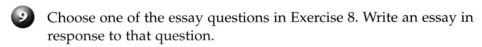

9 Choose one of the essay questions in Exercise 8. Write an essay in response to that question.

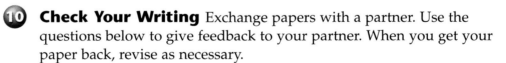

10 **Check Your Writing** Exchange papers with a partner. Use the questions below to give feedback to your partner. When you get your paper back, revise as necessary.

- Can you identify the type of essay?
- Does the essay answer the question effectively?
- Are the language and grammar accurate?
- What was unclear about the essay?
- What was interesting about the essay?

GETTING STARTED

Warm Up

1 What do you think the expression "rules were made to be broken" means? Do you ever ignore any rules of your school, workplace, or community? Discuss your answer with a partner.

2 Which of these two statements do you agree with more? Why?

    a. The main purpose of laws is to protect people.

    b. The main purpose of laws is to control people.

3 Listen to the conversation between two roommates about their neighbor. What is the problem? What solutions do the men mention? What do you think the men should do?

Figure It Out

4 A radio talk show host is interviewing a legal expert about concepts of law. Read their interview.

> **HOST:** Welcome to "Counselor's Corner." Today we're talking with noted legal scholar Hanna Marquez. OK, let's start at the beginning. So, Dr. Marquez, why do we have laws anyway?
>
> **DR. MARQUEZ:** Well, basically laws help people live together. They're a written code of conduct that's been formally agreed on in a society. Laws provide a means of settling disputes.

5

HOST: Laws protect the rights of the individual, don't they? I mean, if a child gets threatened by another child, laws protect the child being threatened, right?

10 **DR. MARQUEZ:** Yes, that's right, but we shouldn't assume that all laws are based on protecting individual rights. The law *protects* the individual, as in the case of the threatened child, but laws also *control* the actions of individuals, in the case of the child who does the threatening. However, not all legal systems 15 are based on individual rights. Some are based on the rights of the family or society.

HOST: Yeah, but the rights of the family are just the same as rights of the individuals in the family, aren't they?

DR. MARQUEZ: No, not necessarily. The needs of an individual may 20 conflict with those of the family or group. In several legal systems, the needs of the family take precedence over those of the individual.

HOST: I'm not sure I follow you. Can you give us an example?

DR. MARQUEZ: OK, for instance, families usually share basic resources like 25 food and shelter. This isn't a problem when these resources are plentiful. When they're scarce, however, it's a different matter, and people have to make some hard decisions. For example, in the past, the Athabascan people of Alaska used to abandon sick or elderly family members when food ran 30 short. This way they made sure that the younger, healthier members of the family could live on. The survival of the family was 35 considered more important than that of the abandoned individuals.

HOST: This is fascinating. I know that you have lots more 40 information for us. Let's go to the phone lines and take calls from the audience.

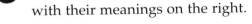

5 **Vocabulary Check** Match the words and expressions on the left with their meanings on the right.

_____ **1.** noted (line 2)

_____ **2.** code of conduct (line 5)

_____ **3.** means (line 6)

_____ **4.** take precedence (line 21)

_____ **5.** elderly (line 29)

a. get involved

b. famous

c. be more important

d. set of rules for behavior

e. method or way

f. people who are old

Talk About It

 A trial lawyer and her assistant are discussing an upcoming murder trial. Work with a partner. Take turns being the lawyer and the assistant and discussing the concerns below. Use the conversation as a model.

Example: preparations for the case

ROLES	MODEL CONVERSATION	FUNCTIONS
Assistant:	Well, we're pretty well-prepared for this one, aren't we?	Ask for confirmation of a statement.
Lawyer:	Yes, we sure are—as ready as we'll ever be.	Confirm or deny the statement.
Assistant:	You have all the documents, don't you?	Ask for confirmation.
Lawyer:	Of course—they're right here in my briefcase.	Confirm or deny.

Legal Concerns

a. evidence from the scene
b. the client's testimony
c. the jury selection

d. their chances of success
e. the length of the trial
f. (your own idea)

GRAMMAR

Tag Questions

When we want to confirm that we have understood something correctly, we can use tag questions. In a tag question, a statement is followed by the auxiliary verb and the pronoun associated with the subject. If the statement is affirmative, the tag is negative; if the statement is negative, the tag is positive. We also use expressions such as *right* or *OK* as tags. Tags are rarely used in written English.

> **Laws have** existed for thousands of years, **haven't they**?
> Most **laws aren't** universal, **are they**?
> **Laws vary** from country to country, **don't they**?
> A country's laws **can** be confusing, **can't they**?
> Some laws are based on precedent, **right**?

The preferred answer to tag questions is the same as in the statement.

> **A: You're** a lawyer, **aren't you**? (I'm fairly sure you **are** a lawyer.)
>
> **B:** Yes, I am.   **OR**   No, I'm not actually. (I'm not a lawyer.)
>
> ---
>
> **A: You're not** a lawyer, **are you**? (I'm fairly sure you're **not** a lawyer.)
>
> **B:** No, I'm not.   **OR**   Yes actually, I am.

In informal language, some tag questions use plural verbs or pronouns which disagree with the forms used in the statement. Moreover, when we are discussing a group of people (*everyone/anyone/someone*), we sometimes use plural pronouns in the tag.

> **I'm** the only real witness, **aren't I**?
>
> **Everyone/anyone/someone can** legally buy cigarettes, **can't they**?
>
> **No one should** be kept in prison indefinitely, **should they**?

1 A student in a political science class is talking with her professor. Complete the dialogue with the correct tag questions.

STUDENT: If laws help us live with one another, then that means people who live outside of any society, don't need laws, **(1.)** _____?

PROFESSOR: Well, actually, yes . . .

STUDENT: Take hermits, for example. They live completely alone, **(2.)** _____?

PROFESSOR: Yes, but . . .

STUDENT: In that case, if there aren't any other people around, no one would be hurt or disturbed by a hermit, **(3.)** _____?

PROFESSOR: Now, this is a tough question. As a matter of fact . . .

STUDENT: Well, anyway, not everyone will agree that hermits don't need laws, **(4.)** _____? Maybe we all need a different kind of law. We probably need a set of internal laws . . .

PROFESSOR: Uh, huh . . .

STUDENT: I mean, these should guide us in making difficult decisions, **(5.)** _____? But I don't think they can be based on religious or moral principles, **(6.)** _____?

PROFESSOR: Now that you mention it . . .

STUDENT: Now that I think about it, many legal systems *have* been based on religion, **(7.)** _____—like the laws of the Catholic Church in Europe in the Middle Ages. There were a lot of systems in place when I was born, **(8.)** _____? They were established many, many years before I was born, **(9.)** _____?

PROFESSOR: That's a very interesting subject . . .

STUDENT: Oh, thank you so much for all your help! I've asked a lot of questions, **(10.)** _____? But, I'm going to remember all of this later, **(11.)** _____?

PROFESSOR: I certainly hope so.

2 Work with a partner. Take turns making assumptions about each other using tag questions.

Example: lawsuit

A: You've never been sued by anyone, have you?

B: Actually, I have. A woman slipped on the ice in front of our house and sued us, but she lost.

a. marital status
b. family
c. work or school
d. car
e. traffic ticket
f. (your own idea)

Participial Phrases

One way to shorten clauses is to use present participles in modifying phrases. This reduction is only possible when the subject of the dependent clause is the same as the subject of the main clause.

Complete Sentence	Reduced Sentence
While he was waiting for the trial to start, **the attorney** looked through his notes.	**Waiting** for the trial to start, **the attorney** looked through his notes.
Because they had already met with the judges, **the attorneys** knew what to expect.	**Having already met** with the judges, **the attorneys** knew what to expect.
While the defendants were coming into the courtroom, **the audience** got quiet.	(No change possible because the subjects are different.)

3 Rewrite the sentences using participial phrases. Some sentences cannot be reduced. Compare your answers with a partner's.

a. Because they needed a way to settle disputes, societies developed trials.

b. As these trials took many different forms, they were unusual by contemporary standards.

c. Because they had committed serious crimes, some defendants were thrown into a river.

d. Because they hadn't drowned in the river, the attorneys proclaimed them innocent.

e. While the innocent died, the guilty lived.

f. Because they needed to be punished, the guilty were then killed by other means.

Expressions of Contrast and Concession

Some conjunctions express differences (contrast), others contrast two ideas that may both be true (concession). Expressions of concession often show that there are unexpected connections between two ideas.

Expressions of Contrast
(but, while, whereas, however, in contrast, on the other hand)

> **While** some laws protect individuals, others protect society.
> Some laws protect individuals. **In contrast**, other laws protect society.

Expressions of Concession
(although, but, yet, even though, though, even so, however, nevertheless, nonetheless, on the other hand, despite, in spite of)

> **Although** the man pleaded his innocence, he was taken into custody.
> The man was taken into custody **despite** his pleas of innocence.
> The man was guilty; **nevertheless** he was set free.

---

 4 **Check Your Understanding** Complete the conversation below using expressions of contrast or concession. Compare your answers with a partner's and explain your choices.

CALLER: I heard about a woman who spilled hot coffee on her legs. She sued the fast food place for a lot of money and won! Isn't that ridiculous?

MARQUEZ: **(1.)** _____ you've got some of the facts of the case, you don't have all of them. This particular restaurant was serving coffee that was twenty degrees hotter than the usual temperature. They had received over 700 complaints about the coffee; **(2.)** _____, they refused to lower the temperature of the coffee they sold.

CALLER: So, you mean, **(3.)** _____ the complaints, this place was still serving coffee they knew was too hot?

MARQUEZ: Precisely. The company had also already paid $500,000 to settle customer complaints about coffee temperature, **(4.)** _____ the company didn't make any changes.

CALLER: Wow. I didn't know that. Still, why did the woman get so much money?

MARQUEZ: The coffee burns caused the woman to spend a week in the hospital; part of the money went to pay her medical expenses. **(5.)** _____ the jury awarded the woman $2.7 million as a punishment to the company, a judge later reduced the fine to $480,000.

CALLER: OK, so the company was partly responsible for the accident. **(6.)** _____, wasn't the woman also partly responsible? After all, everyone expects coffee to be hot, don't they?

MARQUEZ: Absolutely. The woman was held partly responsible for the accident, **(7.)**_____ she was the victim, because she was careless with the coffee. She was awarded less money because of her part in the accident. You've brought up some good points, and we *could* focus only on the money. **(8.)**_____, we could focus on the fact that, because of this case, the wrongdoer compensated the victim and changed a dangerous practice so that others wouldn't get hurt in the same way.

☑ ⑤ **Check Your Understanding** Complete the sentences using the words in the parentheses and your own ideas.

    a. The restaurant continued to make very hot coffee
    (even though) _____

    b. The jury awarded the woman 2.7 million dollars
    (despite) _____

    c. The woman was responsible in some way
    (nonetheless) _____

⑥ **Express Yourself** Work with a partner. Discuss the case above or another case of your choice. Contrast the responsibility of all parties involved. Then share your results with the class.

    Example: A woman sued an airline for ruining her vacation when her flight was cancelled.

LISTENING and SPEAKING

Listen: Office Hours

① **Before You Listen** Who makes international laws? What happens when an international law is broken?

STRATEGY **Listening for Analogies** When listening for understanding, effective listeners listen for any analogies that a speaker might use to help explain a difficult concept. In an analogy, an unfamiliar or difficult idea is compared with a familiar idea.

② Listen to a conversation between a student and a professor. As you listen, pay attention to the analogy that the professor uses and complete the sentence. Compare your answer with a partner's.

The professor compares _____ to _____.

3 Listen again, and take notes to answer the following questions.

   a. How, according to the student, is international law different from domestic law?

   b. What example does the student give of something that could go wrong?

   c. Why would a strong country agree to play by the rules even if it didn't have to?

Pronunciation

Intonation in Tag Questions

Intonation in tag questions is important because the same tag can have a different meaning depending on its intonation. If you are not sure of the truth and you want more information, you use rising intonation for the tag, as you would in a yes/no question.

   • You were alone in the store, weren't you? (↑)

   • You didn't know where to hide it, did you? (↑)

However, if you are almost certain that what you are saying is true, and you expect the listener to agree with you, you use falling intonation as you would in a statement.

   • You were alone in the store, weren't you? (↓)

   • You didn't know where to hide it, did you? (↓)

---

4 Predict whether the intonation of each tag in each dialogue is rising or falling. Mark an **X** in the correct column.

	Rising	Falling
1. A: You heard what happened in your uncle's store yesterday, **didn't you**?	____	____
B: No, actually, I didn't.		
2. A: You were the only one in the store when the money was stolen, **weren't you**?	____	____
B: No! Don't say that! I didn't take the money!		
3. A: Admit it. You robbed your uncle, **didn't you**?	____	____
B: No! I told you before. I didn't take the money!		

  5 Listen to the dialogues to check your predictions.

6 Work with a partner. Take turns reading the dialogues, focusing on the intonation of the tag questions.

Speak Out

 Reviewing Discussion Skills (3) Coming to a decision in a discussion is not always easy. You may propose a solution yourself, or analyze someone else's. You may support a colleague's suggestion, or be asked a question you are not prepared to answer. These interactions are often part of the decision-making process.

Proposing a Solution	Analyzing a Solution
A: And now let's hear from Kate.	**A:** David's idea makes a lot of sense, don't you think?
B: Well, I have an idea I think will work. I've made a flow chart that will help you see where I'm going. Here.	**B:** While it appears insightful at first glance, I see two potential problems.
Evading an Answer	**Offering Support**
A: What weaknesses do you see in Hank's proposal?	**A:** What do you think, Steve?
B: I haven't fully explored all the information yet. I'll get back to you.	**B:** I'm completely behind Kate's solution. It's both timely and cost-effective.

7 Decide if these expressions are **E** (evading an answer), **O** (offering support), **P** (proposing a solution), or **A** (analyzing a solution).

_____ **a.** I'd like to offer a suggestion, if I may.

_____ **b.** There's really no definitive answer.

_____ **c.** Taking a look at the pros and cons . . .

_____ **d.** There are several drawbacks to consider here.

_____ **e.** Ana is right on target—that's the right idea.

_____ **f.** I'll research that and let you know.

8 Work in a small group. Take turns discussing the topics. Use language appropriate for evading answers, proposing a solution, analyzing a solution, and providing support.

- judging minors as adults
- limiting damages
- the death penalty
- dismissing cases on technicalities
- plea bargaining
- (your own idea)

READING and WRITING

Read About It

1 **Before You Read** People talk about the letter of the law (what the law actually says) and the spirit of the law (the intention of the law). Can someone maintain the letter of the law and yet break the spirit of the law? Discuss with a partner.

Categorizing Examples When reading for critical analysis and creative action, it is important to analyze the examples used to support the ideas. Examples can clarify an idea, or introduce a broader topic, which will encourage the reader to explore the topic in depth. Examples can serve as illustrations of a point, as models to follow, or as springboards to creative action.

2 Read the article. As you read, pay attention to how the writer uses examples to support the broader topic.

Informal vs. Formal Traffic Laws
By Dan Keegan

A traffic ticket and a criminal record for driving at the speed limit? How could anyone be charged with obeying speed limit laws?

With a sign protesting the 100 km/h (62 mph) limit fixed to his car, Ontario teacher Gordon Thompson and a friend drove side by side at exactly the limit on
5   Ontario's Highway 401. Between them they created a moving roadblock that infuriated some drivers to the extent that they passed on the shoulders. Every now and then, the duo pulled off to relieve the pressure, but they kept this up for over 80 km (50 miles) on what is one of the province's major arterial roadways.

They were charged with obstructing the highway and public mischief. The
10 latter, a criminal offense, was later dropped in return for pleading guilty to the obstruction charge. Both wound up with a fine and a six-month license suspension. After the trial, a prominent lawyer noted that, in his opinion, Mr. Thomson should have only been fined $100 at most for being a
15 "left-lane bandit" and that his friend should not have been charged with anything.

The roadblock was Thompson's protest against being fined for doing what drivers do all the time on this stretch of highway—drive at 115 to120 km/h,
20 (71 to 74 m/h), the difference being that Thompson knew the police were behind him. They'd tolerated the 110 to112 km/h (68 to 69 m/h) Thompson said he was traveling at for the previous 10 km. When he pushed the speedometer needle up towards 120,
25 the flashing red lights went on.

However, it's obvious that Thompson's strict obedience of the law wasn't the real issue here, or the source of the charges. There was much more to this incident than being a left-lane bandit or merely driving too slowly for traffic conditions. The real issue was Thompson's challenge to what traffic
30 sociologist J. Peter Rothe calls "the moral order of the roadway," the system of trust and expectations that allows drivers and other road users to interact with one another efficiently in the everyday practical circumstances of driving. What Thompson and his friend did was engage in a conspiracy to disrupt the delicate balance between the written law and the moral order.

35 A delicate balance

In this moral order, traffic laws coexist with informal rules in a sort of symbiotic relationship that helps traffic to work efficiently and adapt to situations. The unspoken, undefined nature of these informal rules makes them difficult to discuss and deal with. For police, the written laws are often a tool for enforcing 40 the informal rules and maintaining the checks and balances of the system.

A "zero tolerance" enforcement of traffic laws is hardly possible, much less desirable. We humans are not that clever at devising rules to cover all situations at all times, and sticking strictly to the rules, as unions have found out, is a good way to bring a system to its knees. Instead, we allow individuals to improvise, 45 and they do. But, as Rothe points out, these improvisations are not whimsical or unordered. "Driving," he says, "includes standardized behavior that is at the root of all community living." People don't live by following rules exactly, but neither do they make up their behavior as they go along.

On the roadway, Rothe notes, "cars, lanes, intersections, roadway markings, 50 signal lights, and traffic signs are interpreted according to the significance they have for people's driving purposes." And while there's lots of individualistic behavior, people generally follow norms. This allows for smooth performances as drivers and other road users communicate with one another and negotiate their way through everyday interactions in traffic.

55 The smooth performer

The very smooth performer is the one who has mastered all the skills involved in control, tactics, communicating, making decisions, and managing the subtle interactions of traffic with the least amount of physical and social friction.

Naturally, these norms develop somewhat differently according to culture 60 and place, and even from locality to locality. Sometimes the differences are so subtle that drivers moving from one area to another are irritated or distracted by them without being able to figure out why. Montreal drivers complain about Toronto's bad driving, and vice versa. Vancouver drivers have their own unique style of interaction.

65 Drivers learn to play the game. Gordon Thompson's protest was a direct challenge to this game. His goal was to prove that the speed limit doesn't work, but it does—not by making everyone drive at 100 km/h or less, but by shifting the balance of roadway power from those who want to drive at 120 towards those who want to drive slower.

Reprinted from Drivers.com courtesy of PDE Publications.

 Work with a partner and answer the questions.

a. In this article, what was the letter of the law? What was the spirit of the law? Which did Thompson break? How?

b. What examples of "informal and formal traffic laws" did the author use?

c. What examples does the author cite for standardized behavior on the roadway? Did these examples explain, give models, or were they used as springboards?

Think About It

 In your opinion, do police more often enforce the spirit of the law, or the letter of the law? Why do you think this is true?

Write: Writing an Opinion Essay

Sometimes essay questions specifically ask students to express an opinion. In opinion essays, the writer's opinions are expressed in a thesis statement and are supported by reasons and examples.

STRATEGY There are two basic approaches to writing an opinion essay: the deductive approach and the inductive approach. In a deductive approach, the writer states his or her opinion in the introductory paragraph and supports it with reasons and examples in the supporting paragraphs. In the concluding paragraph, the writer summarizes his or her opinion and support.

In an inductive approach, the writer introduces the various aspects of the topic in the introductory paragraph and discusses each aspect in the supporting paragraphs. In the concluding paragraph, the writer states his or her opinion.

Write About It

 Choose a topic below and write an opinion essay on it.
   a. Should safety gear (seat belts and bicycle helmets) be required by law?
   b. Should students be required to wear uniforms?
   c. Should military service be mandatory?
   d. Should trials be decided by juries or judges?

  Check Your Writing Exchange papers with a partner. Use the questions below to give feedback to your partner. When you get your paper back, revise as necessary.

- Is there an introductory paragraph with a thesis statement?
- Do the supporting paragraphs support the thesis?
- Is there a concluding paragraph?
- Are the grammar and language accurate and clear?
- What do you like about the essay?
- What would you like to hear more about?

GRAMMAR

IDENTIFYING AND CORRECTING ERRORS: The purpose of this question type is to demonstrate your ability to identify errors and correct them as you would in correcting an essay you have written. The errors in this kind of task can involve a verb, a preposition, or any part of speech. Before answering each question, read each answer choice.

A Circle the error and correct it. Write the correction on the line. If a word needs to be deleted, write it on the line and draw a line through it.

1. Nightmares are dreams which can cause <u>so</u> strong feelings of distress <u>that</u> the
                                        A   B

   dreamer often feels <u>very</u> anxious even after awakening <u>in spite of</u> being aware
                             C   D

   that he or she was only dreaming.

   CORRECTION: _____

2. A dreamer may feel <u>as many</u> different types of negative emotions in a nightmare <u>as</u>
                             A   B

   he or she feels in waking life, <u>such like</u>, depression, sadness, anger, or guilt, <u>but</u> in
                                          C   D

   most cases dreamers report feeling anxious and afraid.

   CORRECTION: _____

3. <u>While</u> many nightmares involve the dreamer running away from someone or
    A

   something, <u>either</u> that person <u>or</u> the thing <u>are</u> often unknown to the dreamer.
                     B   C   D

   CORRECTION: _____

4. The dreamer may attempt to call out for help repeatedly, making actual groaning

   noises which, <u>although</u> usually not <u>very</u> loud, are sometimes <u>enough loud</u> <u>to</u> be
                     A   B   C   D

   heard by someone else sleeping nearby.

   CORRECTION: _____

5. Anyone can have a nightmare, <u>and</u> it is thought <u>that</u> probably everyone <u>has</u>
                                A   **B**   **C**

    nightmares at some point in their lives, <u>even so</u> they might not remember having them.
                                                 D

    CORRECTION: _____

6. Although nightmares <u>or</u> night terrors can occur at any age, <u>but</u> nightmares in
                             A   **B**

    particular occur most often in children of approximately three to eight years old,

    and not <u>so</u> often in children younger or older than that age, <u>unless</u> a child has
           C   **D**

    experienced a traumatic event.

    CORRECTION: _____

7. Neither young adults nor old adults <u>has</u> as <u>many</u> nightmares <u>as</u> children typically
                                         A   **B**   **C**

    have. <u>Nonetheless</u>, studies show that it is possible that almost 10% of adults have
           D

    nightmares fairly regularly.

    CORRECTION: _____

8. No one is <u>very</u> sure what causes nightmares <u>although</u> it is known that stress,
                A   **B**

    certain medications, and illnesses can trigger nightmares <u>so much</u> <u>as</u> a traumatic
                                                  C   **D**

    event of one sort or another can.

    CORRECTION: _____

9. Nightmares caused by an event traumatic <u>enough</u> <u>for</u> <u>to</u> cause severe distress, <u>such as</u>
                                             A   **B** **C**   **D**

    in an earthquake, can recur over a long period of time.

    CORRECTION: _____

10. <u>But</u> some therapists believe that these nightmares might help the dreamer to heal
     A

    psychologically, <u>although</u> <u>in the event of</u> the nightmares recurring for too long,
                    B   **C**

    <u>instance</u> beyond a few months, this may not be the case.
       D

    CORRECTION: _____

ANSWERING GAP-FILLING TASKS: The purpose of a gap-filling task is to allow you to demonstrate your ability to identify the missing word(s) from the context and to supply the correct grammatical form in the blank. Many standardized tests present gap-filling tasks. Some tasks target specific grammatical points and some put a gap at every seventh (more or less) word. To complete this task, read the entire passage first. Then, go back and choose the correct word(s). Your choice should make sense, and be grammatically correct.

B Fill the gap with the best word from the box.

too	neither	very	while	having	however
thinking	although	additionally	nor	unless	or

(1.)_____ television was first used by a U.S. president as an advertising medium in the late 1930s, it was not used again that way for another decade. (2.) _____ already accustomed the American public to listening to him on the radio, President Roosevelt felt that television was the natural next step. (3.)_____, the advent of World War II prevented television from developing as it should have.

In 1948, when television began to grow in popularity, Republican nominee, Thomas Dewey was advised that (4.) _____ he used television in his campaign against Harry S. Truman, he might not win. (5.) _____ there weren't even one million televisions in America at that time, Dewey's advisors felt that television advertisements would reach a key part of the population and help him keep the lead. (6.) _____ that his lead against Truman was strong enough to win with just a low key campaign, Dewey ignored the advice. Actually, (7.)_____ Truman (8.) _____Dewey used television advertising in their campaign. Dewey felt strongly that advertising himself on television was (9.) _____ undignified.

COMPLETING DIALOGUES: The purpose of this gap-filling task is to allow you to demonstrate your ability to use tag questions based on the context. Some standardized tests target specific grammatical points for gap-filling.

C Complete the dialogue with tag questions.

A: Did you say people were interested in lawyers and law cases these days?
B: Yes. There are a lot of TV shows, (1.) _____?
A: Yes, there are, but there are lots of shows on TV about lots of other things, too.
B: I didn't say law shows were the only kind, (2.) _____?
   All I said is that people are very interested in the law and lawyers.
A: I guess you're right. There's always at least one court case on.
B: Hey, for a change, let's get a video to watch tonight. What do you want to see?
A: We could get *Presumed Innocent*, (3.) _____?
B: Yeah. That's a good idea. I'm just in the mood for a good legal mystery.

VOCABULARY

> **ANSWERING VOCABULARY QUESTIONS** This task demonstrates your ability to use different forms of a word. You do not need to know the meaning, you need to know how the word fits into the sentence grammatically. Make sure you use prefixes and suffixes to complete this task.

A Read the paragraph. Change the grammatical form of the words in parentheses to complete the sentences.

For a new law to be **(1. formal)** _____ approved, it must go through several different review bodies. Each review body represents a **(2. criticize)** _____ stage in the approval process. Widely divergent viewpoints may be **(3. manifest)** _____ during discussion at each stage. Sometimes longwinded discussion and disagreement amongst legislators can seem to **(4. paralysis)** _____ the process. This process can require a great deal of patience and well-thought out responses. It is certainly no place for **(5. nerve)** _____ dispositions.

B Read the sentences. Change the grammatical form of the words in parentheses to complete the sentences.

1. We read an article comparing the dreams of specific members of a target group with the **(normal)** _____ which have already been established.
2. It is hard not to wonder if the celebrities who make **(endorse)** _____ truly like, and actually use, those particular products.
3. Do you think it is **(ethic)** _____ for the tobacco companies to target teens in their ad campaigns?
4. When **(stereotypical)** _____ are used widely in advertising, they can have an adverse effect on society.

WRITING

> **ANSWERING ESSAY QUESTIONS** Many standardized tests require test takers to demonstrate their ability to write an essay. Read the topic carefully and make a brief outline of how to answer the question. Begin writing your answer. Be careful with time. Try to allow yourself time to read over your essay to correct any errors in grammar, spelling, or punctuation.

Write a persuasive essay in response to one of the questions below. Allow yourself no more than thirty minutes. Be sure to include an engaging introduction and conclusion in your essay and support your ideas with examples.

1. Should advertising of alcohol and cigarettes be permitted on television?
2. Should we use our dream interpretations to help us make decisions about our waking life?
3. In a court of law should the accused be considered innocent until proven guilty, or guilty until proven innocent?

GETTING STARTED

Warm Up

All of us have trouble communicating with people at times. Sometimes these difficulties are not caused by the words we use but by the messages we communicate nonverbally.

1 Look at the pictures above. What is the relationship between each pair of people? How can you tell? Discuss your ideas with a partner.

2 Listen to the following statements. Do they match the pictures above? Why or why not? Discuss your ideas with a partner.

Figure It Out

3 A proverb states what we *don't* say is often more important than what we do say. Read this article on nonverbal communication and find out how.

Body language—posture, gestures, touching, and facial expressions—communicate beyond cultural boundaries. Nonverbal language is complex and subtle. Nonverbal language can completely wipe out the messages of speech. Albert Mehrabian and S. R. Ferris found that when something is expressed
5 through facial expression or body gesture *and* simultaneously through contradictory spoken words, the receiver will react almost entirely to the nonverbal message. For example, if a talker says, "Shut your mouth!"

(continued on next page)

or, even more rudely, "Drop dead!"— and if that slashing command is tempered by even the faintest smile, the message will be read not as what the words say,
10 not even as a confusing or mixed message, but as an expression of humor and affection. The nonverbal language vetoes and transforms the verbal. The opposite, however, is generally not true; words rarely cancel a message the body sends.

Like knowing any language, understanding the rudiments of body language can be valuable to anyone, for either "reading" or "talking." Everyone "reads" some
15 amount of body language, picking up messages on at least an unconscious level. Becoming more conscious of it as a language is bound to increase anyone's "reading" accuracy. The other side, of course, is that fluency in body language can enable anyone to use it for sending powerful messages that instill impressions, that persuade, that cover and conceal attitudes and feelings a person may not
20 wish to reveal. Yes, body language, the great truth-teller, probably can be used by an unusually skilled practitioner as a tool of concealment and deceit.

  Vocabulary Check Work with a partner. Use the context of the reading to discuss possible meanings of the following words.

a. boundaries (line 2)   c. slashing (line 8)   e. vetoes (line 11)
b. wipe out (line 3)   d. tempered (line 8)   f. picking up (line 15)

Talk About It

 A friend from another country is visiting. Work with a partner. Take turns being the guest and the host, and discuss the appropriate gestures. Use the conversation as a model.

Example: signalling a waiter in a restaurant

ROLES	MODEL CONVERSATION	FUNCTIONS
Guest:	How do I signal a waiter in an American restaurant?	Ask about a gesture.
Host:	You should raise your hand and try to make eye contact.	Answer the question.
Guest:	Can I snap my fingers?	Ask about the appropriateness of another gesture.
Host:	No, it'd be considered rude to do that.	Indicate the appropriateness.

Gestures

a. asking for the check in a restaurant
b. expressing "I don't know"
c. wishing someone good luck
d. indicating a a small amount of something
e. indicating victory
f. (your own idea)

Passive Modals

To emphasize that an action is more important than the person or thing doing the action, we use the passive voice. Modals can be used in the active and the passive voice. To form a negative, use *not* after the first auxiliary or modal.

	Passive Voice
Present	(modal + *be* + past participle) **A:** How do you indicate the number one? **B:** Either the thumb or the index finger **may be raised** to indicate "one."
Past	(modal + *have* + *been* + past participle) **A:** I never thanked the staff at the hotel for cleaning the room. **B:** Your thanks **could have been expressed** by leaving a tip. I'm sure that **would have been appreciated**.
Present Progressive	(modal + *be* + *being* + past participle) **A:** Does raising your thumb still indicate that everything is OK? **B:** I think so. That gesture **should** still **be being used**.
Past Progressive	(modal + *have* + *been* + *being* + past participle) **A:** Why was everything covered in white cloth? **B:** I don't know. White cloth **could have been being used** to indicate mourning.

1 Complete the sentences with the appropriate verb forms.

Some personal characteristics **(1. may, indicate)** ＿＿＿＿＿ by the direction in which people turn their eyes when they are thinking about something challenging. Verbal skills **(2. can, associate)** ＿＿＿＿＿ more strongly with left-gazers than with right-gazers, while mathematical skills **(3. can, correlate)** ＿＿＿＿＿ more with right-gazers. As expected, left-gazers **(4. may, find)** ＿＿＿＿＿ more often in humanities classes and right-gazers in mathematics classes. A left-gazer **(5. might, hypnotize)** ＿＿＿＿＿ more easily and have a more vivid imagination.

This study, like most psychological studies, **(6. can, express)** ＿＿＿＿＿ in terms of "tendencies." Some people **(7. can, observe)** ＿＿＿＿＿ to be more consistent in turning their eyes one way or the other. The characteristics attributed to one type **(8. might, show)** ＿＿＿＿＿ by the other, since many factors determine the classes people take. The subjects **(9. can, choose)** ＿＿＿＿＿ from a group that, coincidentally, had these characteristics in common. Like most psychological studies, this **(10. can, not, expect)** ＿＿＿＿＿ to be completely accurate.

2 Use the information below each sentence to complete the sentence. Use the passive voice in the present tense.

a. In Korea, _____ with both hands.
   business card/should/present

b. In Japan, _____ without comment.
   business card/must not/put away

c. In Saudi Arabia, _____ until all
   dinner/may not/serve
the guests have arrived.

d. In Germany, usually _____
_____ .
   business executive's first name/should not/use/a junior colleague

e. In Turkey, _____ to anyone, as
   the bottom of your shoe/must not/show
this is considered to be an insult.

f. In the United States, _____ off the
   elbows/ought to/keep
dinner table.

g. In Thailand, _____
   conversation/may/suspend/diners
until after a meal is eaten.

A modal may have more than one meaning, and more than one modal may express a similar meaning. For example, *may* and *might* express both **permission** and **possibility**.

Permission	Possibility
May I ask you a question?	He **may gesture** to let us know when he has finished speaking.
Might I have a word with you?	That face he's making **might mean** he's unhappy or that he's in pain.

3 Fill in the blanks with the function from the box that best describes the purpose of the sentence.

ability	(present)	obligation	(present)
possibility	(past)	permission	(present/future)
advice	(present)	regret	(past)
strong belief	(past)		

a. May I ask you a question? _permission (present)_

b. Should you dress conservatively if you have an interview at a conservative company? _____

c. Wilson might have been offered the accounting job if he hadn't dyed his hair orange before the interview. _____

d. He can do the job as well as anyone else can. _____

e. The interviewers must not have liked his unconventional hair. _____

f. He should have been better coached on what to wear to the interview. _____

4 Circle the words in parentheses that best complete the sentences.

Faces and bodies **(1. can carry/can be carried)** so many messages that we even **(2. notice/are noticed)** when a statue or drawing **(3. seems/is seemed)** dull and lifeless. **(4. Imagine/Be imagined)**, then, the difficulties that **(5. faced/were faced)** by the creators of *Shrek*, a full-length, computer-animated movie. They **(6. had to use/had to be used)** computer commands, not muscles or drawings, to help the characters communicate nonverbally.

Previous computer-animated movies, such as *Toy Story* and *Antz*, **(7. featured/were featured)** toys and ants, respectively, neither of which **(8. used/was used)** many facial expressions. In *Shrek*, humans, a human-like ogre, and a very expressive donkey **(9. featured/were featured)**. In order to give the illusion of life, these characters **(10. had to portray/had to be portrayed)** with appropriate gestures and facial expressions. For example, the characters **(11. smiled/were smiled)**, **(12. frowned/were frowned)**, **(13. cried/were cried)**, and **(14. showed/were shown)** other emotions through their faces and their bodies. The supervising animator of *Shrek* **(15. said/was said)** that the hardest part of doing the animation **(16. had to have been/had to have been being)** when Shrek **(17. was trying/was being tried)** to hide his emotions.

  5 **Express Yourself** Work with a partner. Describe the characters and plot of a movie, a TV program, or a short story using both the active and the passive voice. Share your descriptions with another pair.

LISTENING and SPEAKING

Listen: Choosing an Executive Assistant

1 **Before You Listen** What do you think executive assistants in a company do? In what ways might they communicate nonverbally? Why might their nonverbal communication be important? Discuss your answers with a partner.

STRATEGY **Listening for Expressions of Contrast or Concession** When giving opinions, people state both positive and negative points. When listening for understanding, it is important to listen for expressions that emphasize contrast (*but, while, whereas, however, in contrast, on the other hand*) or concession (*admittedly, granted, to tell the truth*), which signal to the listener that the speaker may be expressing both positive and negative opinions.

 2 Listen to a conversation about choosing a new executive assistant. Then write the positive and negative characteristics of each candidate in the chart below.

Candidate	Positive	Negative
Ronaldo		
Teresa		
LaTanya		

3 Listen again and answer the questions with a partner.

    a. In your opinion, who should be hired? Why?

    b. What advice about nonverbal behavior could be given to someone interviewing for a job?

Pronunciation

Consonant Contrasts Consonant contrasts are very important in English pronunciation because many words in English differ by only one consonant sound. Study the examples.

doze	those	sick	thick	cheese	she's	chip	ship
lead	read	cheap	jeep	Jerry	Sherry	pat	bat
law	raw	eye	high	fun	pun	bent	vent

4 Work with a partner. First, **A** reads the sentences below and **B** circles the words on page 54. Then **B** reads the sentences at the bottom of page 54 and **A** circles the words below.

A reads	A listens and circles	
1. I really don't think that's right.	**1.** watch	wash
2. After I went to the gym for the first time, I was sore.	**2.** sheep	Jeep
3. The ball hit her in the shin.	**3.** raise	race
4. I thought we had a new bet.	**4.** bill	pill
5. I didn't know you were going to buy those.	**5.** heating	eating

Speak Out

 Reviewing Discussion Skills (4) As a discussion progresses, potential conflicts may appear. An effective discussion leader allows for the polite expression of strong feelings and then reduces tension by refocusing the participants on the work at hand. At the end of a discussion, the leader summarizes what the group has accomplished, states unfinished business, and plans the next meeting.

MANAGING CONFLICT	CLOSING A DISCUSSION
Expressing Strong Feelings Politely I feel very strongly about this issue. I have to say that I completely disagree with this because . . .	**Summarizing Work Accomplished** Summing up, we've agreed that . . . In conclusion, I'd like to go over what we agree on.
Diffusing Tension and Refocusing We'll accomplish more if we step back and take another look at our objectives. Your comment is important, but we need to consider . . .	**Making Future Plans** Next time, we'll continue working on . . . At Friday's meeting, we'll need to talk further about . . .

5 Label the expressions **E** (expressing strong feelings politely), **D** (diffusing tension and refocusing), **S** (summarizing work accomplished), or **M** (making future plans).

_____ **a.** I'm sorry, but I'm very upset by this because . . .

_____ **b.** Next week we'll deal with our annual report.

_____ **c.** I understand how you both feel, but we have to . . .

_____ **d.** Wrapping up, we've collected and analyzed the data, and assigned sections to different people to write.

_____ **e.** I really must protest strongly because . . .

_____ **f.** Let's take a deep breath and start over.

_____ **g.** So far, we've decided that . . .

_____ **h.** It looks like we still need to discuss . . .

_____ **i.** I sincerely feel we're on the wrong path here.

_____ **j.** I acknowledge your concerns, and I know you want the best for us, but we have to consider . . .

6 Work in small groups. Take turns using the topics below to develop discussions. Use language for expressing strong feelings politely, diffusing tension and refocusing, summarizing, and making future plans.

- cultural differences in body language
- popular people read facial expressions skillfully
- cultural differences in physical distance between speakers
- nonverbal communication between spies
- (your own idea)

READING and WRITING

Read About It

1 **Before You Read** When talking with someone you don't know well, how far away do you stand? What about when talking to a good friend or when talking to someone you don't like?

STRATEGY **Personalizing** Writers often use examples from their own experience to illustrate their points. When reading for personal interpretation, effective readers connect these points to their own experiences. Personalizing new information in this way makes it more meaningful and memorable.

2 Read the selection. As you read, try to produce your own examples that illustrate the author's point.

Space Speaks
By Edward T. Hall

Spatial changes give a tone to a communication, accent it, and at times even override the spoken word. The flow and shift of distance between people as they interact with each other is part and parcel of the communication process. The normal
5   conversational distance between strangers illustrates how important the dynamics of spatial interaction is. If a person gets too close, the reaction is instantaneous and automatic—the other person backs up.
10   And if he gets too close again, back we go again. I have observed an American backing up the entire length of a long corridor while a foreigner whom he considers pushy tries to catch up with him. This scene has been
15   enacted thousands and thousands of times— one person trying to increase the distance in order to be at ease, while the other tries to decrease it for the same reason, neither one being aware of what is going on. We have here
20   an example of the tremendous depth to which culture can condition behavior.

One thing that does confuse us and get in the way of understanding cultural differences is that there are times in our own culture when people are either distant or pushy in their use of space. Therefore, we simply
25   associate the foreigner with the familiar; namely those people who have acted in such a way that our attention was drawn to their actions. The error

(continued on next page)

is in jumping to the conclusion that the foreigner feels the same way the American does simply because his overt acts are identical.

This was all suddenly brought into focus one time when I had the good
30 fortune to be visited by a very distinguished and learned man who had been for many years a top-ranking diplomat representing a foreign country. After meeting him a number of times, I had become impressed with his extraordinary sensitivity to the small details of behavior that are so significant in the interaction process. Dr. X was interested in some of the work several
35 of us were doing at the time and asked permission to attend one of my lectures. He came to the front of the class at the end of the lecture to talk over a number of points made in the preceding hour. While talking, he became quite involved in the implications of the lecture as well as what he was saying. We started out facing each other and, as he talked, I became
40 dimly aware that he was standing a little too close and that I was beginning to back up. Fortunately, I was able to suppress my first impulse and remain stationary because there was nothing to communicate aggression in his behavior except the conversational distance. His voice was eager, his manner intent, the set of his body communicated only interest and eagerness
45 to talk. It also came to me in a flash that someone who had been so successful in the old school of diplomacy could not possibly let himself communicate something offensive to the other person except outside of his highly trained awareness.

By experimenting, I was able to observe that as I moved away slightly,
50 there was an associated shift in the pattern of interaction. He had more trouble expressing himself. If I shifted to where I felt comfortable (about twenty-one inches), he looked somewhat puzzled and hurt, almost as though he were saying: "Why is he acting that way? Here I am doing everything I can to talk to him in a friendly manner and he suddenly withdraws. Have
55 I done anything wrong? Said something that I shouldn't?" Having ascertained that distance had a direct effect on his conversation, I stood my ground, letting him set the distance.

 3 Answer the questions. Then, compare your answers with a partner's.

a. According to the article, what gets in the way of our understanding cultural differences between people? What examples does the author offer for this claim?

b. During his conversation with Dr. X, the author felt like backing up. Why *didn't* he back up?

c. Have you ever had an experience similar to that of the author or Dr. X? What was the outcome?

Vocabulary Check Match the words on the left with their meanings on the right.

_____ **1.** override (line 2)
_____ **2.** part and parcel (line 3)
_____ **3.** backs up (line 9)
_____ **4.** stationary (line 42)
_____ **5.** shift (line 50)
_____ **6.** stood my ground (line 56)

a. motionless
b. regarded as more important than
c. change
d. didn't move backward or forward
e. an integral component
f. moves in reverse
g. sways

Think About It

 What is a comfortable distance for you to have a conversation with a close friend? How about with a stranger? Is it ever acceptable to touch the person you're speaking with? If so, when? Where? (on the arm, on the head, etc.)

Write: Writing Under Time Pressure

 Essay exams and in-class writing assignments have time limits. To make the best use of time, it is important to allow time to plan your essay and to check it for errors. Most of your time should be spent on actually writing the essay. When working under time pressure, it usually isn't possible to edit as extensively as you otherwise would.

Editing and Feedback

Effective writers edit for content, organization, grammar, and mechanics. In limited time situations, it is important to ask yourself the following questions.

Content

Is the topic worth reading/writing about? Are the ideas presented logically? Are they relevant? Are the purpose and audience clear?

Organization

Is there an introductory paragraph with a clear thesis statement? Does everything in the essay relate to the main idea? Do the body paragraphs support the thesis with facts, examples, and authoritative opinions? Is there a concluding paragraph?

Style

Is the style appropriate and consistent? Are there varieties of sentence types? Is the vocabulary appropriate?

Grammar

Do the subjects and their verbs agree? Are verb tenses used accurately? Is word order correct?

Mechanics

Are the spelling and punctuation correct?

The same questions can be used when you ask another student (a peer) to read and comment on your paper. In peer editing situations, it is helpful to write your comments directly on the paper and to refer to specific portions of the essay as you do so. This will provide a valuable guide for the writer in revising the essay.

Write About It

 Set a timer for thirty minutes. Choose a topic below and write an essay. Allow time to plan your essay and check for errors.

- Do you agree or disagree with the following statement? *Learning the meaning of gestures is as important as learning the meaning of words.* Support your answer with reasons and examples.

- You have the opportunity to spend some time in another city. Would you rather go to a sporting event, a museum, or a shopping mall? Use reasons and examples to support your answer.

  Check Your Writing At the end of the thirty minutes, exchange papers with a partner. Check your partner's paper carefully for content organization, grammar, and mechanics, using the questions. When you get your own paper back, revise it as necessary.

Partner **B**, use the chart below to complete exercise 4 on page 49.

B reads	B listens and circles	
1. Do you want to watch the baby?	1. light	right
2. Mike said he saw a Jeep in the backyard.	2. sore	chore
3. Melanie is going to race horses.	3. shin	chin
4. I couldn't find my bill.	4. vet	bet
5. Are you heating the soup again?	5. those	toes

AMAZING INVENTIONS

George W. Carver

Alexander Graham Bell

GETTING STARTED

Warm Up

Some inventions and discoveries are famous, and their stories will live forever. Other inventions and discoveries are taken for granted, and their stories may be lost forever.

1 Work with a partner. Make a list of five famous inventors and their inventions or discoveries.

2 Match the inventors on the left with their inventions on the right. Compare your answers with a partner's.

_____ **1.** Marion Donovan   **a.** windshield wipers

_____ **2.** George de Mestral   **b.** the ballpoint pen

_____ **3.** Lazlo Biro   **c.** the light bulb

_____ **4.** Thomas Edison   **d.** Velcro®

_____ **5.** Mary Anderson   **e.** the disposable diaper

                                f. the telephone

3 Listen to the conversation. What did George Washington Carver invent/ discover? Who was helped by his inventions/discoveries, and how?

Figure It Out

4 What are some of the inventions of the 21st century? Read the passage on the next page.

After a year of hype and hoopla over
"Ginger" and "IT," New Hampshire inventor
Dean Kamen finally unveiled "Segway," a
motorized two-wheeled scooter with an ability
5 to balance itself, leaving riders free to focus
on the road rather than on staying upright.

Picture the back end of a child's tricycle,
the steering shaft of a scooter, toss in some
cutting-edge engineering, and you'll have
10 a pretty good image of Mr. Kamen's latest
contribution to human locomotion.

"It's the world's first self-balancing human
transport," proclaims the wiry Kamen. "You
stand on this, it goes. It's like putting on a
15 pair of magic sneakers."

Kamen, whose credits for innovation
include the portable dialysis machine and
a self-balancing wheelchair that climbs
stairs, says other commercial partners will
20 also be testing grounds for his scooters.
Among them are the city of Atlanta,
the National Park Service, several police
departments, and online bookseller
Amazon.com.

25 "The key issue is self-balancing,
achieved by tiny gyros tied to other
systems," says Woodie Flowers, a
professor of mechanical engineering at
the Massachusetts Institute of Technology and a close friend of Kamen. "There's a lot
30 of very elegant engineering in that machine—everything from the tires, motors, and
gearing, to the sensor system."

Nevertheless, Segway's power plant is more ordinary than its pre-release media
hype suggested. No fuel cells or heat-recycling engines here. Instead, motors and
cutting-edge batteries provide the horsepower.

35 A single battery charge can run the scooter for 15 miles over level terrain. And it's
cheap to refuel, using just ten cents of electricity in a six-hour charge, Kamen says.

Segway is the latest invention from Kamen's prolific laboratory, DEKA Research and
Development Corp. near Manchester, N.H. The scooter is an evolution of technologies
developed for "Fred," the self-balancing wheelchair capable of climbing stairs.

 5 **Vocabulary Check** Work with a partner. Use the context of the
reading to discuss possible meanings of the following words.

a. hype (line 1) **c.** cutting-edge (line 9) **e.** gyros (line 26)

b. unveiled (line 3) **d.** locomotion (line 11) **f.** horsepower (line 34)

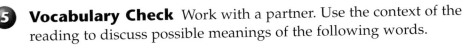

Unit 5

56

Talk About It

 6 Two friends are playing a guessing game about famous people. Work with a partner. Take turns giving clues and guessing about the people below and their achievements. Use the conversation as a model.

Example: a scientist (Marie Curie)

Roles	Model Conversation	Functions
Clue-giver:	I'm thinking of someone whose discoveries were in science.	Describe an inventor or invention.
Guesser:	That could apply to a lot of people. Could you give me another clue?	Make a guess (or ask for another clue).
Clue-giver:	This person, whose achievements included winning two Nobel Prizes, was originally from Poland.	Give another clue.
Guesser:	Is it Marie Curie?	Make a guess (or ask for another clue).
Clue-giver:	Yes, it is.	Confirm the guess (or give another clue).

People

a. an explorer   **c.** an inventor   **e.** a musician

b. a scientist   **d.** a fashion designer   **f.** (your own idea)

GRAMMAR

Relative Clauses: *Whose*

We use the relative pronoun *whose* to show possession. It can be used in both identifying and non-identifying clauses. An identifying clause tells which noun or pronoun we are referring to—it "identifies" the meaning by telling exactly which one(s). A non-identifying clause merely gives more information about the noun or pronoun it modifies. We separate a non-identifying clause from its referent with commas. Identifying clauses do not take commas.

> People **whose only homes were caves** sometimes needed to be inventive in order to survive and pass on knowledge. (identifying clause)
>
> Cave dwellers, **whose only means of writing was with sharpened stones**, drew scenes of their daily lives on their cave walls. (non-identifying clause)
>
> Later, writers began using clay tablets, **whose surfaces they moistened to make them easier to write on**. (non-identifying clause)

1 Read the following statements about using *whose* in relative clauses. Use the examples in the box on page 57 to decide if they are **T** (true) or **F** (false). Compare your answers with a partner's.

_____ **a.** *Whose* cannot modify both people and things.

_____ **b.** *Whose* can be used to modify the subject or object of a clause.

_____ **c.** *Whose* cannot be omitted from the relative clause.

_____ **d.** Both *whose* and the person or thing possessed are placed at the beginning of the relative clause.

2 On a separate piece of paper, combine the sentences to make one sentence using *whose*. Compare your answers with a partner's.

a. People developed symbols instead of pictures to stand for commodities and quantities. These people's jobs were involved with trade.

b. Some of these symbol systems evolved into alphabets. Writers used the alphabets' letters to stand for sounds in the language.

c. The Greek language was the first to be written from left to right. Its writing system was developed around 400 B.C.

d. India ink was invented around 2697 B.C. by a Chinese philosopher. Many people recognize its dark black color.

e. Other cultures also produced colored dyes and inks. The ingredients of these products were made of plants and minerals.

f. For paper, Mediterranean cultures often used papyrus. Its history dates back more than 4000 years.

g. Wood-based paper was not widely used in Europe until the 1400s. The Chinese kept its development secret for about 600 years.

The relative pronouns *which* or *who* can be used as an afterthought to provide additional commentary. This use is common in spoken English.

> My latest invention is a set of onion-chopping goggles, **which should save hundreds of cooks' eyes from onion fumes**. I was inspired by my wife, **who** makes wonderful onion soup.
>
> After I sent that company $5000 to help me market my invention, they never contacted me again, **which, by the way, I think is criminal**.

3 Provide additional commentary with a clause introduced by *which*.

a. Hybrid cars use very little gasoline, _____.

b. Eventually it will be possible to clone human beings, _____.

c. New "wonder drugs" are often quite expensive, _____.

d. MP3 players are the wave of the future, _____.

Reducing Relative Clauses to Phrases

We use *who*, *which*, and *that* as subjects of relative clauses. A clause that contains the passive voice or the progressive form can be reduced to a phrase by omitting the relative pronoun and *be* verb in the clause.

The tires **that were used on early automobiles** were very crude.

The tires **used on early automobiles** were very crude.

The team **that is working on the zero-emissions car** is made up of young engineers from all over the world.

The team **working on the zero-emissions car** is made up of young engineers from all over the world.

---

 4 On a separate sheet of paper, combine the sentences, using phrases instead of clauses wherever possible. Compare your answers with a partner's.

a. The vaccine has saved millions from the dreaded smallpox. It was discovered by Edward Jenner in 1796.

b. I read an interesting article. It predicted inventions of the next millennium.

c. The man told me he had designed a new solar-powered flashlight. He was sitting next to me at the party.

 5 **Check Your Understanding** Complete the paragraph by filling in the blanks with *whose, who(m), that,* or *which*. If you think that nothing is needed, put an X on the line.

People **(1.)**_____ discoveries change the world often start out aiming at something **(2.)**_____ is quite different from what they end up with. Christopher Columbus, for example, **(3.)**_____ was looking for a trade route to East Asia, ended up having a greater impact on history than if he had succeeded in his original goal. When he first bumped into this land mass **(4.)**_____, now called America, he thought he was somewhere else, **(5.)**_____ must have caused some embarassment.

Columbus, **(6.)**_____ dreams were ridiculed by many, may have been a laughingstock at the time, but how many of those **(7.)**_____ mocked him are now remembered?

 6 **Express Yourself** Choose a person whose inventions or discoveries you consider significant, and write a paragraph about him or her. Exchange paragraphs with a partner and discuss them.

Listen: The Miracle Drug

 1 Before You Listen What is penicillin? Have you ever taken it? What is it prescribed for? What do you know about the discovery of penicillin?

STRATEGY **Listening for Sequence of Events and Inference** In narratives, events are not always presented in chronological order. When listening for understanding, it is important to try to determine the sequence of events in order to understand their relationship to each other. In some cases, we can infer that certain events must have occurred, even though they aren't specifically stated.

 2 Listen to a radio interview. As you listen, identify four key events in the development of penicillin. Make an inference about another key event that is not specifically stated, but logically must have occurred.

3 Listen to the interview again, and answer the questions. Compare your answers with a partner's.

Alexander Fleming

    a. The author describes Fleming as lucky. Give two ways in which Fleming was lucky in the discovery of penicillin.

    b. The interviewer spoke of the author's portraying penicillin as a superhero. In what ways is penicillin similar to a superhero?

    c. What do you think the interviewer is going to ask about next? Why?

Pronunciation

Word Stress & Intonation

We use a rising-falling intonation pattern in statements, information questions (*who, what, where, when, why, how,* and so on), and verifying tag questions in which we expect the listener to agree with us.

- **Where** was Ma**rie Cu**rie **ed**ucated?

- **She** was **ed**ucated at the Sor**bonne** in **Pa**ris.

- **She** was a **bril**liant **sci**entist, **was**n't she?

We use rising intonation in yes/no questions, sentences that list items in a series, and clarifying tag questions in which we are not sure of the answer.

- **Did** Ma**rie Cu**rie make many dis**cov**eries? ↗

- **She** dis**cov**ered po**lo**nium, ↗ **ra**dium, ↗ and many **prop**erties ↗ of **ra**dioac**ti**vity. ↘

- **She** had a **daugh**ter, ↘ **did**n't **she**? ↗

4 Predict the stress and intonation patterns in the dialogue. Underline the stressed syllables and draw arrows to indicate the intonation.

A: What were you saying about Marie Curie's daughter?

B: Well, she actually had two daughters. Irene became a scientist who studied radioactivity. Eve became Marie's biographer.

A: The Curie daughters were pretty smart women, too, weren't they?

B: Yes. Marie won two Nobel Prizes and Irene Curie won one, which she shared with her husband.

A: So were Marie's prizes both in biology?

B: No. The first, which she shared with her husband and another scientist, was in physics. The second was in chemistry.

A: The Curies taught at the Sorbonne, right?

B: Yes. When Marie's husband died, she took over his professorship at the Sorbonne, becoming the first woman to teach there.

Marie Curie

 5 Listen to the dialogue to check your predictions.

6 Work with a partner. Take turns reading the dialogue, paying attention to word stress and intonation.

Speak Out

Components of an Oral Presentation Students and professionals are often asked to give oral presentations. A presentation has an introduction, body, and conclusion. We tell our listeners what we're going to talk about, we talk about it, and finally we review what we've said.

Once you know the topic of your presentation, it is important to focus it by determining the purpose and main idea in a preview statement. The preview statement shows your point of view and is supported in the body of the speech.

7 Work with a partner. Identify the introduction, body, and conclusion.

> Can you remember learning to tie your shoes? If you were like me, you struggled a lot. Perhaps because of these early struggles, I really appreciate the fact that Velcro has become an important part of modern life. Today, I want to tell you about the advantages of velcro.
>
> First of all, using Velcro requires less physical agility than other fasteners do. Young children and people with arthritis can secure their shoes easily. Velcro is also easier to manipulate than buttons or zippers.
>
> In addition, Velcro allows for changes. In my mother's company, a message board lets everyone know where each employee is: in a meeting, out of the office, etc. Velcro on the board and on small discs allows the employees to indicate their whereabouts quickly and easily.
>
> These are just two of the many uses of Velcro. I hope that you appreciate how important this simple invention has become. The next time you're looking for new shoes, try some with Velcro fasteners. You'll never go back to laces.

8 For each topic below, come up with a preview statement that introduces the topic. Then give two or three points that will support it.

> - the innovative qualities of a new product
> - the importance of a discovery or invention
> - the dangers of scientific research
> - (your own idea)

9 How would your presentation change if you were talking to a class of elementary school children? Inventors? Government officials? Why?

10 Choose one of the topics and develop it into a short presentation of two to three minutes and present it to a small group.

Read About It

 Before You Read Some inventions have become so common that we rarely think about their impact on our lives. Answer the following questions with a partner: How would your life be different if you didn't have pencils? Paper? Electricity? Telephones? Cars?

STRATEGY **Distinguishing Between Facts and Commentary** In historical and biographical narratives, the main focus is on a presentation of significant facts. However, writers establish their own point of view on these events by blending background information, commentary, and interpretation into the narrative. When reading for critical analysis, an efficient reader needs to be able to distinguish between factual information and the writer's stance on that information.

 Skim through the article. As you skim, try to distinguish between facts and commentary. Put a **C** in the margin of the text next to those sections where you find commentary.

The Pencil
By David Lindsay

In 1565, Konrad Gesner was a medical scholar living in Zurich. Gesner had already written a treatise on the virtues of milk and was moving on to his next attempt: a bibliography of all the recorded knowledge in the world.
5 In the midst of this monumental task, he came across a new kind of writing device, which appeared to be a cylinder of lead sheathed in a wooden case. Who exactly the inventor of the pencil was, Gesner did not say. He simply made a note of it—with his quill, the current instrument
10 of preference—and continued on to the subject of fossils. The following year, he died of the plague.

There is something perfect about this story, with its pairing of small and large. A man sets out to embrace the whole of the human experience and never gets anywhere close, yet the modest object that falls under his gaze goes on to
15 become . . . well, instrumental to the recording of knowledge from that moment on. Explore this loop a little further and the implications turn downright screwy: Gesner was writing about a method of writing, and for as much as he thought he was writing the ultimate document, today a new slew of documentarians (the present author included) are taking their turn in writing about him. The
20 pencil, it seems, is continually creating more work for itself.

The pencil does have a history that moves forward in time and gets somewhere. Its origins lie in antiquity, when Egyptians used a small lead disc for making guidelines on papyrus. (The actual writing was done in ink.) The Greeks

(continued on next page)

later picked up on this practice, as did the Romans, who called the disc
25 a *plumbum*—Latin for *lead*.

Not much happened in the way of pencil technology for another millennium after that. Then, in 1564, (the year before Gesner mentioned the pencil), a deposit of graphite was discovered at Borrowdale in Cumbria [England]. This graphite—called plumbago because it acted like lead—was so solid and
30 uniform that it could be sawed into sheets and then cut into thin square sticks. As the only pure graphite deposit ever found, it also held fantastic financial promise. Less pure deposits of graphite were available in many parts of the world, but they had to be crushed and the impurities removed. And by then the graphite tended to crumble.

35 The Borrowdale mines were active for only six weeks every year, and after the wagons were filled with the stuff, armed guards escorted them to London. Export of the ore itself was prohibited. Instead, it was routed to a newly formed guild—the English Guild of Pencilmakers—which carved wooden cases for the graphite sticks and, in a separate development, enjoyed a world monopoly on the sale of
40 the finished product. Indeed, one could say the English Guild of Pencilmakers was the Microsoft of its day. One could also say that there is a direct line of descent between them: the monopolies of Elizabethan England, most notably the textile monopoly of the Merchant Adventurers, eventually evolved into the joint-stock companies, such as the Virginia Company, that originally footed the bill for the
45 colonization of the New World.

Of course, give people pencils and eventually they'll start to have ideas, no matter how strong your monopoly is. By the seventeenth century, the Germans were using a mixture of graphite, sulphur, and antimony, and the resulting white lead sticks were said to compare favorably with the English pencil. In
50 1779, K.W. Scheele made a chemical analysis of plumbago that proved it to be a form of carbon, not of lead. A decade later, A. G. Werner suggested the more appropriate name graphite, from the Greek word meaning to write. But as is often the case, it took the privations of war to bring about the decisive change.

In 1795, when France was cut off from both the English and German pencil
55 sources, Napoleon commissioned Nicolas-Jacques Conte, an officer in the French army, to develop a viable substitute. Conte mixed powdered graphite with clay and then fired the mixture in a kiln. This method was not only serviceable, but allowed the sticks to be graded from hard to soft by varying the proportion of graphite to clay. When the Napoleonic Wars ended, this new method spread
60 abroad and was eventually adopted by all pencil manufacturers.

In an interesting postscript, the isolation of Napoleon's troops also led to one of the first significant uses of the new pencil. After marching on Egypt, Napoleon decided to withdraw most of his troops but left behind a draftsman named Dominique-Vivant Denon, who proceeded to document the various wonders
65 of that land.

Denon finally returned to Paris and showed his sketches to Napoleon, who liked them so much he appointed Denon as director of the Louvre, which,

not coincidentally, soon housed many of the treasures that Napoleon had looted from
70 Egypt. In time, the Louvre became a favorite location for art students, who faithfully wore down their own pencils sketching these very same treasures. Thus, an Egyptian invention found its way, if not home, at least into
75 familiar surroundings.

 Answer the questions, and discuss your answers with a partner.

a. In line 15, the author uses "...well," Why?

b. A pencil is often called "a writing instrument"; what is the other meaning of "instrumental" that creates a play on words?

c. Where did the author use commentary instead of factual information? What effect did this have on you as a reader of the text?

 Vocabulary Check Match the words on the left with their meanings on the right.

_____ **1.** falls under his gaze (line 14)

_____ **2.** turn downright screwy (line 16)

_____ **3.** slew (line 18)

_____ **4.** crumble (line 34)

_____ **5.** ore (line 37)

_____ **6.** footed the bill for (line 44)

_____ **7.** privations (line 53)

_____ **8.** looted (line 69)

_____ **9.** wore down (lines 71, 72)

a. a large number

b. hardships

c. made smaller through use

d. become very strange

e. paid for

f. covered

g. stole

h. deposit of a mineral

i. is looked at

j. break into small pieces

Think About It

 At one point, the British had a monopoly on pencils. What are some advantages and disadvantages of monopolies? Do you know of any famous monopolies?

Write: Analyzing a Research Paper

The research paper is like a formal essay in which the writer presents a logical argument on an issue or problem. Research papers are expected to have a thesis; there must be a unifying point of view, even in papers that present a factual overview.

 Writers need to refer to authoritative sources, such as journal articles and other current published material. By citing these sources they support the thesis. A list of references cited must accompany the research paper to help readers who may wish to consult the same sources.

6 An analytical research paper examines an issue or problem, breaks it into parts, and analyzes each part closely. Below are elements that are used in research papers. As you read, write the appropriate letter next to the text in the research paper below. Letters can be used more than once, or not at all.

a. thesis statement

b. supporting argument

c. list of parts to be analyzed

d. examples

e. reference to a source

f. list of sources

g. summarizing statement

Implants in the Brain

Loss of sight, hearing, or mobility may seem debilitating, but there is hope for people who have suffered severe nerve damage. This hope comes from computer technology.

If the electrical impulses of the brain were carried through computer circuits instead of damaged nerves, muscles could function. Many people hear better because of cochlear implants, which send messages to the brain (Hockenberry, 2001). A more ambitious project is directly stimulating the brain to respond with the appropriate muscle control. However, these procedures have significant difficulties. We will discuss those obstacles in this paper.

Although the adult brain can continue to learn, it becomes increasingly inflexible over time (Carter, 1998). Therefore, the brain may not make connections, and even if it does, the connections might not yield the intended results. The brain might not understand the new signals (Cerio, 2001).

Another obstacle lies in the nature of the implant itself. The brain is awash in chemicals and electrical impulses, all of which could interact with an implant. In addition, an implant must stay in a designated area while not damaging itself or the brain.

So far, research has been directed toward people who have a physical disability. However, this technology can be taken further. What enhancements could we make to our perception or to our muscle control? What functions will be replaced or circumvented by implants? We may become less dependent on our physical bodies if we can effectively live in our minds because of implants. In the next millennium, man and machine could truly become one.

Carter, R. (1998). *Mapping the mind.* Berkeley: University of California Press.
Cerio, G. (2001, August). Artificial sight. *Discover, 22,* 50-54.
Hockenberry, J. (2001). The next brainiacs. *Wired, 9,* 94-105.

7 Work with a partner. Compare your answers to Exercise 6 and discuss any differences.

GETTING STARTED

Warm Up

Millions of people love to be scared out of their wits. They're hooked on horror.
What is it that makes people so fascinated with frightening things?

1 Work with a partner. How many of these "horrible people" can you
identify? Can you think of others to include in this list?

Stephen King	Bela Lugosi	Mary Shelley
Freddy Krueger	Bram Stoker	Boris Karloff
La Llorona	the Addams Family	Yuki Onna

2 What are some things you are "hooked on"?

 3 Listen to a conversation between two friends. How does each feel
about horror movies? Who do you agree with more? Compare your
answers with a partner's.

Figure It Out

4 What is an "urban legend"? Why are they so popular? Read the article
on the next page and find out.

"Urban legends" are the modern equivalent of the fairy tale. They are used to entertain us and to teach us how to behave in the modern world. These stories don't take place long ago and far away; on the contrary, they have entered our own neighborhoods, our own living rooms, and our own e-mail. One that went
5 international in the late 1990s was about someone who, after spending an evening with a stranger at a party, wakes up in a bathtub full of ice, missing a kidney, with a note taped to a telephone directing the victim to call an ambulance. Urban legends are usually passed from friend to friend,
10 and they are often told at gatherings where each participant is encouraged to contribute to the variations. With the widespread use of e-mail, urban legends are easily passed from one person to many, from continent to continent.

15   Urban legends are characterized by an inability of anyone to verify a witness or the victim in the story. They always seem to happen to a friend of a friend or to have been printed in an unnamed newspaper somewhere. Legitimate newspapers have sometimes been duped into reporting a legend as authentic. A good urban legend sounds plausible enough to be true and strange enough
20 to be unlikely. It is often hard to ferret out the truth, and we seem to enjoy being caught not knowing whether to believe the legends or not.

    Urban legends have a variety of versions, from rather tame to completely gruesome, taking on the characteristics of the place and the fears of the people who live there. For example, one urban legend tells of someone hiding in the
25 backseat of another person's car. The story could be set in Bangkok, Berlin, or Boston, and the victim may come out of the incident unscathed or hurt in a multitude of physical or psychological ways, depending on the culture and personality of the storyteller. The perpetrator may be supernatural (a ghost or demon) or a member of a racial or other demographic group. The reason for
30 the attack could be revenge, initiation into a gang, insanity, or anything else that might frighten the audience. The purpose, beyond giving us a little scare, would probably be to let others know of this particular danger and perhaps to make them take precautions to avoid the same situation.

    Urban legends will probably be with us for a long time to come. Oh, and
35 just in case there is someone out there, keep the doors to your car locked.

☑ ⑤ **Vocabulary Check** Match the words on the left with their meanings on the right.

_____ **1.** duped (line 18)

_____ **2.** plausible (line 19)

_____ **3.** ferret out (line 20)

_____ **4.** gruesome (line 23)

_____ **5.** unscathed (line 26)

_____ **6.** perpetrator (line 28)

    a. not exciting

    b. not harmed

    c. tricked into believing something

    d. believable

    e. person who commits an illegal act

    f. discover through careful work

    g. offensively frightening

Talk About It

 6 A writer and a producer are discussing ideas for a new television program. Work with a partner. Take turns being the writer and the producer and react to the story suggestions below. Use the conversation as a model.

Example: hunting demons

ROLES	MODEL CONVERSATION	FUNCTIONS
Writer:	We could have crocodiles patrol the streets of the city.	Make a suggestion.
Producer:	That's a good idea. We could also have the crocodiles seeking revenge on the hero.	Reject the suggestion, and make an alternative suggestion.
Writer:	Better yet, the crocodiles don't like one another, so we could make them fight among themselves—a sort of crocodile war.	Respond to the suggestion, and make another suggestion.

Story Suggestions

a. investigating alien sitings
b. getting rid of ghosts
c. using ESP to find lost children
d. creating new life forms
e. battling werewolves
f. (your own idea)

GRAMMAR

Causatives: *Have, Let, Make* and *Get*

Study the examples below.

In his 1886 novel *Dr. Jekyll and Mr. Hyde*, Robert Louis Stevenson **got** his audience **to examine** a theme that was somewhat ahead of its time.

In the novel, Stevenson **has** his protagonist, Dr. Jekyll, **struggle** with the dark side of his nature, personified by the evil Mr. Hyde.

Stevenson **lets** the reader **enjoy** the story purely as entertainment.

At the same time, he **makes** the reader **feel** the tension and terror of the divided self.

1 Use the examples in the box on page 69 to decide if the following statements are **T** (true) or **F** (false).

   _T_ **a.** Causatives indicate that someone or something caused a person or thing to do something.

   _____ **b.** All of the causatives are followed by an object and the simple form of the verb.

   _____ **c.** Causatives are only used in the past.

   _____ **d.** *Have, let, make,* and *get* have somewhat different meanings when they are used as causatives.

2 Check the sentences that have a causative in them.

   ☐ **a.** Dr. Jekyll tries to make himself divide into pure good and pure evil.

   ☐ **b.** Mr. Hyde has all the characteristics of evil, but Jekyll can't attain the same state of good.

   ☐ **c.** Stevenson makes Hyde smaller than Jekyll, indicating that, in the beginning, good was stronger than evil.

   ☐ **d.** Stevenson has Jekyll struggle with both good and evil, but he doesn't have Hyde experience the same thing.

   ☐ **e.** As the story progresses, Stevenson lets Hyde grow stronger until Jekyll can no longer control him.

   ☐ **f.** Jekyll has his will drawn up by his lawyer, leaving everything to Hyde.

   ☐ **g.** This makes Jekyll's lawyer suspicious.

   ☐ **h.** By the time the lawyer gets to the heart of Jekyll's secret, it is too late to save Jekyll.

   ☐ **i.** Jekyll gets his friend to keep his secret until after his (Jekyll's) death.

   ☐ **j.** When Jekyll dies, Stevenson has Hyde die, too.

Expressions of Cause and Effect

We signal cause-effect relationship by words such as *so, therefore,* and *as a result.* An effect-cause relationship is indicated by words such as *because, since,* or *due to.*

> CAUSE
> In the 1920s and 1930s, movie studios had to attract and keep audiences,
>
> EFFECT
> **so** they were constantly searching for new genres and stories.
>
> EFFECT   CAUSE
> They had to try to "do more with less," **since** they didn't have large production budgets.

Words and Phrases that Show Cause-and-Effect Relationships		
so	**for this reason*	*as*
in that	*since*	** therefore*
*consequently	*because of*	*due to (the fact that)*
*as a result	*because*	
* = more common in written English than in spoken English		

3 On a separate sheet of paper, combine the sentences, using the expressions in parentheses. Then compare your sentences with a partner's.

a. (since) The studios often took their plots from live theatre. The movies sometimes looked like theatre productions.

b. (therefore) The studios didn't want to offend anyone in their audiences. They used stories from British and American novels, whose content was acceptable to a mass audience.

c. (in that) The films avoided graphic violence. They implied, but didn't show, violent scenes.

d. (as a result) *Dracula* and *Frankenstein* were financial successes. Other studios began to make horror movies.

e. (as) Audiences got tired of the same old thing. The studios tended to use the same techniques and plots again and again.

When we wish to emphasize to what degree something is affected, we use *so* + adjective + *that* or *such* + noun phrase + *that*.

We were **so** scared **that** we screamed.
It was **such** a scary movie **that** we screamed.

4 On a separate sheet of paper, combine the sentences using *so . . . that* or *such . . . that*.

1. The special effects were good. People screamed at what they saw.

2. "Talking movies" were realistic. They were far more effective at scaring people than silent films had been.

3. The films' advertising was dramatic. Moviegoers believed that each new movie would be scarier than the last.

4. Even today, horror films have a large following. They cannot be ignored.

Expressing Purpose

Purpose can be expressed by using *so that/in order that* + clause, or (*so as*) *to/ in order to* + verb.

> Many pre-Christian traditions and symbols were adopted by the medieval Church **so that** people would feel more comfortable converting to Christianity.
>
> During the Middle Ages, gargoyles were incorporated into church architecture (**so as**) **to help** make a bridge between the old religion and the new religion.

 5 Combine the sentences using *so that* + clause, *in order to* + verb, or *so as to* + verb.

Example: Medieval builders often carved Bible stories on the walls of cathedrals. Illiterate people could understand the stories.

Medieval builders often carved Bible stories on the walls of cathedrals*ₐ*illiterate people could understand these stories.
so that

a. These builders made drain spouts at the corners of the cathedrals. They wanted to keep rainwater away from the walls.

b. The drain spouts were sometimes carved in the shape of gargoyles. The buildings were protected from demons as well as from rainwater.

c. Gargoyles were carved in many other places as well. These gargoyles decorated the building.

d. Sometimes builders carved the faces of the gargoyles to look like famous people of the time. The builders wanted to make a political statement.

 6 **Check Your Understanding** Circle the best word or phrase to complete the sentences.

The popular lore about vampires suggests that evil forces possess humans and (**1. make/get**) them to do terrible deeds. This concept is closely related to the idea that the vampire is a blood-drinker who has to have fresh human blood (**2. so that/in order**) to survive. According to legends, vampires were once ordinary mortals who, through their own ignorance, (**3. had/let**) a vampire drink their blood. Now their own bloodlust will not (**4. make/let**) them rest. They, too, must constantly find new victims (**5. so that/such that**) they can continue to live. (**6. Consequently/Because**), the population of vampires will grow unless mortals fight back.

 7 **Express Yourself** Work with a partner and discuss horror movies. What psychological needs do they respond to? Share your ideas with the class.

LISTENING and SPEAKING

Listen: An Interview with a Horror Writer

 1 **Before You Listen** What questions would you ask a horror writer? List five questions. Share your questions with a partner.

STRATEGY **Listening for Supporting Arguments** In conversation, supporting arguments are not always presented in a linear, logical order. When listening for critical analysis, it is important to identify supporting arguments and relate them to the speaker's main points.

2 Listen to a radio interview with a horror writer. As you listen, take notes of both women's opinions and the supporting arguments that each uses to defend her point of view.

3 Listen again and answer the questions. Compare your answers with a partner's.

   a. What is the interviewer's main case against horror stories? What arguments does she use to support her case? How does the horror writer respond?

   b. Who do you agree with more? Why?

Pronunciation

> ### Reduction and Holding
>
> In English, a word sometimes ends in a consonant sound, and the following word begins with the same consonant sound, which is not necessarily the same letter. When this happens, the full consonant sound is not pronounced twice. It is pronounced only once (reduction), but is held a little longer than usual (holding).
>
> • Godzilla, a Japanese fil<u>m m</u>onster, was more than just a huge lizard. (/m/)
>
> • It also served as a reminder o<u>f v</u>arious dangers of nuclea<u>r r</u>esearch. (/v/ and /r/)

4 Predict which letters will be reduced and held by underlining them. Some sentences contain more than one pair.

   a. In 1954, the United States conducted a hydrogen bomb test on Bikini Island.

   b. Although this was just a routine test, in the Japanese movie *Godzilla*, it was presented as an atomic catastrophe that creates a giant mutant lizard.

   c. The later revised version, however, did not tell quite the same story.

   d. Godzilla still demolished Tokyo, but many of the anti-nuclear references were cut.

   e. The original lizard dies in the first film, but in later films, other monsters are created due to other nuclear reactions.

5 Now listen to check your predictions.

6 Work with a partner. Take turns saying the sentences, focusing on holding and reduction.

Speak Out

STRATEGY **Introductions** A good introduction to a presentation has an attention-getting opener and a preview of what will come. To get and keep your audience's attention, you need to open your talk in an interesting way, such as making a provocative statement, telling an anecdote or a joke, asking a question, or giving a quotation.

> * You may think that the Golden Age of Horror has already passed, but I say it has yet to come.
> * When I was young, I always imagined monsters in the bedroom closet. I don't have to imagine them anymore.
> * What is the one thing that scares you more than anything else?
> * "The only thing we have to fear is fear itself." (Franklin D. Roosevelt, former U.S. president)

You need to connect your opener to your preview statement.

> "The only thing we have to fear is fear itself." Obviously, when Franklin Roosevelt said this, he hadn't seen the new movie *Ghostwalk*. [*connection*] This is by far the best horror film in the last five years. It has good acting, believable special effects, and chills, chills, chills. [*preview*]

7 For each preview statement below, develop an opener and connect it to the main idea. Give a preview of the supporting statements. Share your ideas with a partner.

    a. Many horror stories are just not believable.

    b. A little fear is a good thing.

    c. A book is more/less frightening than a movie is.

    d. (your own idea)

Read About It

 Before You Read Most people can only describe a few jobs involved in making a horror movie. Aside from actor, director, producer, and camera person, can you name any other jobs involved in making a movie?

STRATEGY ▶ **Recognizing Tone and Level of Formality** When reading for critical analysis, it is important to note the tone or attitude a writer adopts toward the subject. The language the writer chooses conveys the tone. Colloquial, informal language signals a casual tone, whereas formal language conveys a serious tone.

2 Read the passage. As you read, note the level of formality and the tone used.

Who Are These Guys?
By Dave Kehr

Time was when movies concluded with the words "The End" over the studio logo.

Nowadays the words "The End" are rare, but they have been replaced by many, many others.
5 End credits on movies can run for three to four minutes (usually enough time to perform the title song) and are full of densely packed names, job titles, and acknowledgments. On a major special-effects movie, such as *The Abyss*, the credits can
10 run most of a twelve-minute reel by themselves.

Who are these people, and where did they come from?

A surprising amount of the effort that goes into making a film is devoted to sheer schlepping—to getting what you need to where you need it. Once the location manager finds a shooting site, the transportation coordinator must plan
15 how to move all of the necessary people, equipment, and props to it. He or she will have a fleet of trucks and drivers, complete with captains and mechanics.

Among the first to move is the construction coordinator—with his foreman, purchaser, head (lead) carpenter, and the "hammers," the guys that actually put nails in wood. Once the set is built by the "swing gang," it has to be painted
20 (by the lead painter, standby painter, and sign painter) and "dressed" with props purchased by the buyer, transported and supervised by the leadman (also called the gang boss), and positioned by the dressers and standby dressers.

The crew members associated with the operation of the camera carry the most exotic job titles on the credit list. The key grip is not a tenacious
25 locksmith, but the head (key) of the crew (the grips) in charge of all the non-electric apparatus connected with the camera—the scaffolding that holds

(continued on next page)

it up, the crane that makes it fly, the dolly that lets it move along the ground. The gaffer is the chief electrician, in charge of setting up lights and putting down cables.

30   Both the key grip and the gaffer have assistants, called "best boys" for reasons no one (perhaps thankfully) can seem to remember, who communicate their instructions to the lighting and equipment operators. The camera operator is responsible for the actual care and feeding of a movie's most important piece of equipment and works with his first assistant (called the "focus puller")
35 to keep the lens and shutter properly adjusted and his second assistant (the "loader") to make sure the darn thing has film in it. All of these crew members work under the supervision of the director of photography (or "D.P." as these directors are universally known), who is charged with transforming the director's intentions into reality. Presiding over all of this on-set activity, are the assistant
40 directors, the location managers, the script supervisor, and the production coordinator who reports to the ultimate traffic cop, the production manager.

For the soundtrack, the equivalent of the director of photography is the production sound editor, who, with the help of a team of assistants, (including the boom man, in charge of dangling the microphone just out of camera range)
45 pieces together the final assembly of sound, exclusive of the music. The music is the responsibility of the music editor, who has worked with the composer and a recording engineer to create the music cues requested by the director. The two tracks—sound and music—are finally blended together and balanced for stereo by the rerecording mixer.

50   Meanwhile, the editor, generally working closely with the director, has assembled the image tracks, the negative cutter has duplicated the editor's cut using precious camera negative, and the color timer has adjusted the tone and density of every scene in order to make the colors consistent throughout.

When the soundtrack and the image are finally joined together, what
55 you have theoretically is a movie. Sometimes it's *Citizen Kane*. Sometimes it's *Howard the Duck*.

3 Answer the questions. Work with a partner and compare your answers.

a. What was the main idea of this article?

b. How would you describe the tone of the article? Cite specific examples of language or punctuation from the article to support your opinion.

c. What are the duties of the key grip, the best boy, the gaffer, the focus puller, and the music editor?

Vocabulary Check Match the words on the left with their meanings on the right.

_____ **1.** run (line 5)

_____ **2.** densely (line 7)

_____ **3.** acknowledgments (line 8)

_____ **4.** swing gang (line 19)

_____ **5.** boom man (line 44)

_____ **6.** range (line 44)

_____ **7.** blended (line 48)

_____ **8.** tone (line 52)

a. distance something can be seen

b. constructs movie sets

c. installs lights and cables

d. mixed together, joined

e. list of contributors

f. thickly, closely

g. shades of color

h. in charge of the microphone

i. continuing to go on

Think About It

5 Which, if any, of the jobs do you think you might be interested in? Discuss in small groups.

Write: Choosing and Narrowing a Topic

 An analytical research paper presents facts in an authoritative and persuasive way. To write one, you should first select a topic you know something about, and most importantly, one that evokes a strong reaction in you. You need to narrow your topic by focusing on an aspect that can be fully discussed.

Then, you analyze the narrowed topic, research it, and come to a reasoned opinion about it. Your essay should reflect your ideas after you have carefully thought and read about the issue; it should not be just a collection of quotations or paraphrases of other people's ideas. Your viewpoint on the topic is your *thesis*. The purpose of your paper is to persuade the reader of the validity of your thesis. Your thesis should be stated in the introduction to your paper.

6 Discuss with a partner how the items in the list can help you choose and narrow a topic.

- the reference section of the library
- tables of contents of books or magazines
- a weekly current events magazine
- textbooks
- computer search engines
- teachers, classmates, friends, parent
- electronic encyclopedias

Answer these questions. You may want to use some of the items from Exercise 6 to help you.

    a. What general topic are you interested in?

    b. What specific aspect of this topic are you concerned about?

    c. What do you already know about this topic?

    d. How can your topic be discussed from different perspectives? For example, how can it be discussed from a sociological, psychological, historical, technological, biological, or a personal perspective?

    e. What point of view do you want to convince your readers of?

    f. What will the thesis, or main idea, of the essay be?

In most of the remaining units of this book, you will concentrate on the different aspects of writing a researched analytical essay, sometimes called a modified term paper. You will write a paper longer than the model in Unit 5, and it will be based on your stance and on the research you have done on your topic. For this reason, it is important that you choose your topic well.

 Generating and Organizing Ideas Once you have decided on the topic of your paper, you need to generate and then organize ideas for it. There are several strategies that can help you do this. Brainstorming is useful for getting started. For organizing and clarifying your thinking, try using time lines or idea maps.

As a final step before you begin writing, a formal outline is recommended. This can serve as your guide as you compose and revise your paper.

Write About it

 Begin generating and organizing your ideas for the topic that you have chosen. Develop an idea map and an outline for your topic. Your idea map may contain more ideas than you will actually use in your paper; you can narrow your focus as you create your formal outline.

  Check Your Writing When you have finished, exchange your idea map, and outline with a partner. Comment on your partner's work. When your work is returned to you, revise as necessary.

PROGRESS CHECK

GRAMMAR

IDENTIFYING UNNECESSARY WORDS: You may be asked to identify unnecessary, or irrelevant, words in a text. In this type of question, not every sentence contains a mistake. The most common errors are unnecessary articles, pronouns, and prepositions, or incorrect comparisons. When you see these words, be sure to check if they belong in the sentence.

A Decide which sentences are correct and which have an incorrect additional word. Circle the incorrect word. Write C on the line for correct sentences.

_____ 1. Some studies show that 93 percent of communication is (more) nonverbal.

_____ 2. Business people who they are working with people from other cultures need to be aware of the differences in nonverbal communication.

_____ 3. There are some gestures which will not mean anything to people from the other cultures.

_____ 4. Moreover, some gestures which are considered rude in one culture may be commonly used in other cultures.

_____ 5. Misunderstandings caused by the misinterpretation of nonverbal communication signals can to cause costly mistakes for international business people.

ASSESSING ANSWERS: Check that each of the choices can fit grammatically into the sentence and eliminate those that do not. Then look at the subject of the sentence and make sure that the choices refer to the same subject. Be sure to answer every question. If you do not know an answer, use your instincts or guess.

B Circle the letter of the word that best completes the sentence.

1. Chester Greenwood was only a boy of fifteen when he created his first invention, earmuffs, _____ he could protect his ears while working outside in the cold.   A (B) C D
   (A) so as   (C) such that
   (B) so that   (D) in order

2. At the time, he was inventing a new type of ice skates and the earmuffs _____ out in the cold longer.   A B C D
   (A) let him stay   (C) made him able
   (B) get him warm   (D) have him stand

3. Chester's earmuffs earned him a fortune during World War I, _____ was strange because they are really only a simple invention to keep ears warm.   A B C D
   (A) what   (C) which
   (B) get him warm   (D) whose

4. Although Chester also invented other things, it was the ear muffs which _____ him recognition and a parade in his hometown.   A B C D
   (A) had   (C) let
   (B) got   (D) made

5. The local police cars in this parade were decorated as giant earmuffs _____ remind everyone of Chester's main contribution to the town of Farmington, known as the earmuff capital of the world.

   A B C D

   (A) so as   **(C)** because of

   (B) so that to   **(D)** in order to

6. Chester's first invention _____ his most important one, but it is the one he is best remembered for in his hometown.

   A B C D

   (A) may not have be   **(C)** may have not been

   (B) may not have been   **(D)** may not have being

7. Chester was only fifteen, but the youngest person to ever get an invention patented was a four-year old girl _____ invention helped people with arthritis to be able to handle doorknobs.

   A B C D

   (A) who's   **(C)** whose

   (B) while   **(D)** who has

8. Perhaps we should all _____ the ideas of small children a bit more seriously!

   A B C D

   (A) take   **(C)** to take

   (B) look   **(D)** been taking

> **STRATEGY** **ANSWERING LIMITED PRODUCTION QUESTIONS** You may be asked to fill in missing words to test if you can produce correct answers as well as recognize them. It is important to read the entire text first for general understanding. Then decide what type of word goes in each gap. Fill in the words you know first, then return to those you are not sure of.

C Fill in the gaps in the following sentences with an appropriate word.

I love horror movies so **(1.)** _____ that I spend a great deal of my free time watching them, **(2.)** _____ is a bit foolish, but I can't seem to help myself. I watch them primarily **(3.)** _____ I like the way they **(4.)** _____ me experience frightening events while feeling completely safe. Watching horror movies **(5.)** _____ me feel as if I have experienced something extraordinary. **(6.)** _____, I am more able to appreciate the wonderfully ordinary qualities of my own life. Occasionally I feel as if my time **(7.)** _____ to have **(8.)** _____ spent in a more productive manner, but if we were always doing only what we should **(9.)** _____ doing, there **(10.)** _____ be enough fun in life, in my opinion.

VOCABULARY

ANSWERING WORD FORMATION QUESTIONS Some exams test your ability to change words so that they fit into a sentence grammatically. Make sure you examine the sentence to determine what part of speech (noun, verb, adverb) is needed to fill the blank before you change the word. Review the suffixes so you can use the base form to create other parts of speech.

A The words on the right can be used to form a word that fits in the blank grammatically. Complete each sentence with the correct form of the word.

Horror books have been a hot trend for teens and preteens for several years. Although at first this concerned many parents, their concerns were **(1.)** _____ by the discovery **OVERRIDE** that these sometimes gruesome stories were being read by their children who would normally have preferred to **(2.)** _____ on a plate of spinach and broccoli than **MUNCH** read a book. Some teachers also **(3.)** _____ their **VETO** students reading horror books at first, but their objections were soon **(4.)** _____ by the large numbers of students **WEAR DOWN** who were **(5.)** _____ of reading as a result of **FALL UNDER THE SPELL** reading these horror stories. Almost anyone would agree that whatever it is that **(6.)** _____ a love of reading in **INSTILL** children is worth its weight in gold. It wasn't long before horror books were **(7.)** _____ into school libraries. **FIND THEIR WAY** Although many of these books are a far cry from quality literature, it is hoped that as the children grow, their interests will **(8.)** _____ to reading other types of books. **SHIFT**

B Circle the letter of the word(s) which can best replace the boldface words in each sentence.

1. A carefully chosen tone of voice combined with appropriate eye contact and body language can mask just about any type of **deceit**.   A B C D
   (A) feeling   **(C)** dishonesty
   (B) assumption   **(D)** manipulation

2. Even something completely absurd can be made to sound **A B C D**
    plausible if said with the right combination of tone of voice
    and confident eye contact.
    (A) valid   (C) sincere
    (B) honest   (D) believable

3. One of the many voice qualities which appears to be universal **A B C D**
    is the rising intonation used when asking a *yes/no* question.
    Researchers believe this is because the higher register **tempers**
    the request for information.
    (A) softens   (C) clarifies
    (B) conceals   (D) disguises

4. It would be useful to find a way to deliver an unwelcome message **A B C D**
    in an **overt** way that didn't offend or anger anyone by changing your
    tone of voice appropriately.
    (A) open   (C) forceful
    (B) hidden   (D) friendly

WRITING

> **ANSWERING ESSAY QUESTIONS** The writing sections of standardized tests are graded on a
> number of criteria. Two important criteria include having an essay that is well-organized,
> and free from grammatical mistakes. Make sure you spend some time creating an
> outline so your essay will be organized. You should always have a clear introduction,
> body, and a brief conclusion. Then, in writing your essay, play it safe. Stick to the
> grammar and vocabulary you know so there will be fewer mistakes. Use a combination
> of long and short sentences when possible.

**Write an essay in response to one of the questions below. Allow yourself no more
than thirty minutes. Be sure to include all the components of an essay.**

A. Do you think it is possible to train people to be inventors in training schools?
B. Do you think the violence in horror stories effects people adversely? If so, how,
   and if not, why not?
C. Do you think students of a foreign language should learn the nonverbal
   communication signals, as well, and if so, how and of which culture?

A HARD ACT TO FOLLOW

GETTING STARTED

Warm Up

Learning is a lifelong endeavor. Our parents are our first teachers. Sometimes, however, we prefer to do our learning on our own and make our own decisions.

1 Which of these topics are you willing to accept parental advice on? Rank them from **5** (very willing) to **0** (not willing at all). Compare your rankings with a partner's.

_____ **a.** clothing style   _____ **d.** spouse

_____ **b.** friends   _____ **e.** music

_____ **c.** school/college   _____ **f.** career

2 Other than parents, who or what helped you to decide on a career? Who might ask you for help one day?

3 Listen to the talk on choosing a career. According to the speaker, how do parents influence our career choices? Discuss your answer with a partner.

Figure It Out

Tedros Mambile, a career counselor, is giving a seminar on choosing careers.

Welcome to Careers for You! I'm Tedros Mambile, your coach, and I'm sure that by the end of the seminar, you'll be headed toward a new and envigorating career!

Before we begin our work, let me tell you about a client of mine. He was a fairly
5 typical student in his last year in high school. His parents were after him to apply to engineering schools; his grandparents on his father's side suggested that he take a year off from school to travel; his mother's parents offered him an entry-level position in their company, with the implied promise that he would run the company when they retired.
10 And if that wasn't enough, his friends wanted him to play the drums in their band. So, you can see, he was under a fair amount of pressure from different sources to choose a particular career.

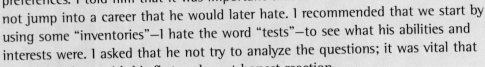

So he came to me. I suggested that he begin by
15 looking at himself to discover his own talents and preferences. I told him that it was important that he not jump into a career that he would later hate. I recommended that we start by using some "inventories"—I hate the word "tests"—to see what his abilities and interests were. I asked that he not try to analyze the questions; it was vital that
20 he answer them with his first and most honest reaction.

What did we learn? We discovered that he had a real knack for working with his hands. We also saw that he was good at managing his own time and that he was a fairly independent worker. He had been nursing an ambition to work as a mechanic in his neighbor's garage, but he hadn't told anyone.

25 As we make our way through the course, I'll tell you more about what happened to this fellow. We'll go through our own process of discovery today, so I request that you try to keep an open mind. It is essential that you listen to yourself and think about your own wants and needs. I'm here to help you do just that.

 4 **Vocabulary Check** Work with a partner. Use the context of the passage to determine the meanings of the following expressions.

- **a.** were after him (line 5)
- **b.** run the company (line 9)
- **c.** jump into (a career) (line 17)
- **d.** have a knack for (line 21)
- **e.** nursing an ambition (line 23)
- **f.** make our way through the course (line 25)
- **g.** keep an open mind (line 27)

Talk About It

5 A career counselor is giving advice to a young client. Work with a partner. Take turns being the career counselor and the client, and discuss career options. Use the conversation as a model.

Example: study law or medicine

ROLES	MODEL CONVERSATION	FUNCTIONS
Client:	My parents want me to study law or medicine, but I'm really not sure if I want to do either one.	State a problem.
Counselor:	Those are good careers, but they can be really stressful. It's important that you consider your parents' wishes, but it's also important that you go into a career where you'll feel comfortable.	Advise the client. Tell what is important or essential.
Client:	So what do you propose I do?	Ask for further advice.
Counselor:	I recommend that you talk to some people in law or medical school, give it some thought, and then talk it over with your parents.	Recommend some options.

Career Choices

a. take over the family business or become an artist

b. become a police officer or a firefighter

c. study information technology or the humanities

d. go into show business or become a teacher

e. (your own idea)

GRAMMAR

The Subjunctive: Expressing Urgency, Necessity, or Advice

We use the subjunctive (the simple form of the verb) in noun clauses following verbs of urgency, necessity, and advice, such as *demand, insist, suggest,* and *recommend.* It is impossible to know if the action in the subjunctive will ever happen. The present subjunctive form is the base form of the verb for all persons or *be.* The negative form is *not* + simple form of the verb. The passive form is *be* + past participle.

Career counselors <u>suggest</u> that people **be** aware of their own skills and preferences.

Her parents did not <u>insist</u> that she **study** in a certain field.

My parents <u>demanded</u> that I **not rule out** college, but they never actually forced me to continue my education.

I <u>asked</u> that advice **not be given** to me unless I asked for it.

The subjunctive is used in noun clauses following *it* + a form of *be* + an adjective of urgency or importance.

While <u>it's important</u> that people **consider** their own talents and desires, <u>it's</u> also <u>essential</u> that they **not forget** the needs of their families.

<u>It is vital</u> to me that my family **not be** totally **excluded** from my deliberations.

1 Fill in each blank with an appropriate verb from the box. Use the subjunctive negative or passive forms as needed.

ask	be	cheat	consider	determine	do	give	pay	take

It is important that you **(1.)** _____ your personality when you are choosing a career. If you have an outgoing personality, you probably won't be happy with a job in which you work mostly by yourself. I recommend that you **(2.)** _____ a personality test to help you understand what jobs you would be best suited for. I also recommend that you **(3.)** _____ when taking any kind of career test because you will only hurt yourself. If it is essential to an employer that you **(4.)** _____ willing to follow rules and **(5.)** _____ questions, then you shouldn't apply for the job if you are always trying to do things in your own way.

Years ago, it wasn't considered essential that an employee **(6.)** _____ happy at work, especially when the work involved manual labor. It was important that the work **(7.)** _____ and that the employee **(8.)** _____. Nowadays, however, studies show that an employee is more productive when she is working at a job for which she is well suited. Some companies insist that job applicants **(9.)** _____ a personality test before they are hired in order to determine the fit between the applicant and the job. If you can't take a personality assessment, it is critical that you at least **(10.)** _____ your strengths and weaknesses so that you don't end up in a career you're unhappy with.

2 Complete the sentences with ideas of your own. Compare your sentences with a partner's.

a. When thinking about a career, it is essential that _____ .

b. You should expect that your parents will suggest that _____ .

c. Your teachers might recommend that _____ .

d. It is important that you not _____ .

e. A potential employer might require that _____ .

f. Your friends might ask that _____ .

☑ ③ **Check Your Understanding** Check (✔) the situations below in which you are *most likely* to use the subjunctive form.

_____ **a.** You are seeking advice from a career counselor about an important job interview next week.

_____ **b.** You are discussing what information is critical to include in a college application with an academic advisor.

_____ **c.** You are talking with a bank manager about what you need to disclose to get a loan.

_____ **d.** You are talking to students who will be spending a year in your country. Give them tips.

④ **Express Yourself** Work with a partner. Choose one of the situations above and write a dialogue. Perform your dialogue for another pair.

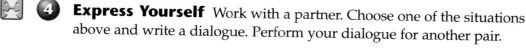

LISTENING and SPEAKING

Listen: Two Roommates Talking

① **Before You Listen** If you were to write your memoirs now, who would you describe as the most influential person in your life? Why? Discuss your answer with a partner.

STRATEGY ▶ **Listening for Excerpts and Summaries** When people talk about other people's writings, they might read an excerpt—or passage—from the work in question, or they might summarize the work in their own words. When listening for critical analysis, effective listeners pay attention to excerpts and summaries in order to get a better sense of the work being described.

 ② Listen to a conversation between two roommates. As you listen, pay attention to the excerpt and the summary, and answer the questions.

a. From which book is there an excerpt?

b. What does the excerpt describe?

c. What points are mentioned in the summary?

③ Listen to the conversation again. How are the approaches of Kingston's mother and Pinkwater's father different? How would your parents react in similar situations? Share your ideas with a partner.

Pronunciation

Sound-Spelling Dissimilarity (1)

Often the same vowel sound will have several different spellings in English.

/ɔ/	/i/	/e/	/u/
off	he	bed	use
bought	sea	head	you
taught	eat	guess	boot
draw	meet	egg	threw

4 Predict the pronunciation of the vowel sounds of the words by putting them into the appropriate columns in the chart.

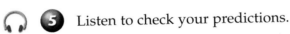

blue
breath
broad
caught
chief
cough
draw
fence

grew
group
lead
read
seek
steps
through
wealth

bought /ɔ/	beat /i/	bet /e/	boot /u/

5 Listen to check your predictions.

6 Work with a partner. Take turns pronouncing the words in the chart, focusing on the sound-spelling links.

Speak Out

STRATEGY **Using Visual Aids** Effective speakers use visual aids to accompany their presentations. Visual aids help speakers organize their information, and they help the audience understand and remember that information. Visual aids may be an outline of the main points, a list of bulleted points, a graphic, a picture, or an object. You can use a PowerPoint presentation, a flip chart, a chalkboard, transparencies, or handouts for your visual aids.

7 With your partner, discuss each of the points about effective visual aids. Why is each point important? Can you think of others?

   a. Be sure your visual aids, including printed material, are large enough for people in the back of the room to see them.

   b. Keep your visual aids very simple, not cluttered or complicated.

   c. Don't hand out papers or pass around objects while you are speaking.

   d. Maintain eye contact; don't speak to the board or screen with the visual aid on it.

   e. Only show the part of the visual aid you are discussing.

Read About It

 Before You Read The reading is a conversation between Raven, a Native American man, and Tilo, a woman from India. What differences in their backgrounds would you expect? What similarities? Discuss your ideas with a partner.

STRATEGY **Reading Conversations** When reading for understanding, it is important to note the quotation marks and the context to determine which character is speaking. When a conversation is presented in a text, quotation marks are used to mark where a character starts and stops talking. A change in speaker is usually indicated by a change in paragraph, but when a speaker continues over more than one paragraph, the end quotation mark is not used until the speaker is interrupted or stops speaking. Each new paragraph, however, starts with quotation marks to indicate that the previous speaker is continuing.

 Read the selection. As you read, pay attention to who is speaking. Write the name of the speaker in the margin next to each paragraph.

The Mistress of Spices

by Chitra Banerjee Divakaruni

"I came to tell you the rest of my story. If you have time."

"The best time I'll ever have," I say, and he begins.

5 "The death of my father cut me free of all ties, all caring. I was like a boat that had come unmoored, bobbing in an ocean filled with treasure troves and storms and sea monsters, and who knew where I would end up?

10 "Have you ever felt this way, Tilo? Then you know what a lonely feeling it is, and how dangerous. It can turn men into murderers, or saints.

"I had no one to love, for in their different 15 ways both my father and mother were lost to me—and my great-grandfather too, though I was careful not to think of him. And so the laws of this world no longer seemed to apply to me. The opinions of others meant nothing. 20 I felt light and porous, as though I could become anything I wanted—if I found something worth being—or implode into nothingness. "I spent a lot of time alone in bed, staring at the ceiling, imagining possible 25 lives. My present existence—scraping through classes, getting in fights, partying with the guys, sitting at the dinner table with my mother, swallowing forkfuls of silence— filled me with dissatisfaction. There was no 30 direction to it, no intensity. No *power*.

"For slowly it came to me as I lay in my room while outside the world rushed by that there was only one thing in life worth having. Power. It was what my great- 35 grandfather had offered me in that dying room. It was what my mother had snatched from me. And though I could never go back to *that* moment, *that* power, there

(continued on next page)

were other kinds in the world. I needed to
40 find the one that would be right for me.

"I toyed with wildly different thoughts—
becoming part of a gang, going off with the
Peace Corps, joining the army. Even going
back to that clapboard house to find
45 someone who knew my great-grandfather's
ways. But in the end I did none of them. In
the end I went to business school.

"You're laughing? I knew you would. But this
is what came to me as I lay wondering:
50 money was at the center of the world—at
least the one I lived in. Money was power.
With money I could remake myself—not like
my poor mother strained to do, but
completely, suavely, at once and forever.

55 "For the most part I was right.

"The finances were not a problem—my
father had had life insurance—but I knew
I'd have to work hard and change my
habits—pull up my grades, quit hanging
60 around with the guys, things like that.
But it was less difficult than I'd thought.
I discovered an unexpected hardness in
myself, a drivenness, something that shook
off all that could hold me back, something
65 that didn't mind cutting through all that was
in the way. Maybe it was a quality I'd got
from my mother, but in the passing down it
had crystallized, grown more adamantine.

"My days took on a silent, submarine
70 quality as I prepared myself for my future.
People receded from me, and I let them
go gladly. The friends who scoffed or tried
to incite me to fight, the teachers who
discussed me in amazed whispers in the
75 staff lounge, even my mother who watched
me thankfully but without understanding.
They were merely distractions, ripples
on a distant surface which had little
to do with my life. I would feel the same
80 way about my classmates in college.

"This is what I discovered about myself
in college: I understood money effortlessly,
its strange logic. How it came, how it grew,
its ebbs and flows. I delighted in its secret
85 language. I had a knack for investments,
and even in those first days—I was still a
student—when I started playing the market,
I knew exactly what to buy and when to sell."

"And did it bring you the power you
90 dreamed of?"

My American looks down at the lines of his
hands, then into my eyes. "It brought me
power, yes. And a—*solidity*. I could see
why in the old tales the giants were always
95 counting their gold. It assured them that
they were real. There's a headiness to
money-power, the feeling that everything
in the world is there for you to pick up and
examine, choose or discard, like you might
100 do with fruit at a produce stand. And you'll
be amazed at how many things you can
buy, and people too. I'd be lying if I said
I didn't enjoy that.

"From the beginning I decided that I'd
105 have fun with my money. I gathered
around me all the things I thought would
bring me that fun. You would probably
think them infantile, coming as you do
from a less materialistic culture."

110 I let it pass. Another time, Raven, I think, we will discuss this...

"I realize now that they were a poor boy's fantasy of the rich life, gleaned from glossies and TV shows. Yachts, penthouse
115 apartments, Porsches, Gucci underwear, vacations on the Riviera or at Vegas. All the stereotypes. People who've always been rich probably spend their money quite differently. But I didn't care, and none of the
120 new friends (if you could call them that) who gathered around me seemed to mind."

"What about your mother?"

Sharp silence, like a shard of glass between us. Then Raven says, "When
125 I made my first million, I sent my mother a check for a hundred thousand dollars. It was the first time I'd corresponded with her since I left home. Oh, she'd write to me, not often but regularly, telling
130 me what she was doing. Nothing exciting—church bazaars, planting petunias in the spring, getting the house painted, things like that. After a while the letters would come and I'd leave them unopened.
135 Sometimes they'd get misplaced before I read them. I never wrote back.

"Why should I, I told myself. There's nothing between us anymore. But I think I wasn't quite honest with myself. Somewhere in the
140 back of my mind I wanted to show her that I'd done what she wanted to better than she ever had. I'd made it in a world she couldn't even dream of being part of. That's why I sent her the check, and with it a
145 photo of myself and a bunch of friends—including my latest girl—at a beach house I'd just bought down in Malibu. It was to be

the ultimate punishment."

He gives a harsh laugh. "Well, the letter
150 came back with a red stamp saying they couldn't find anyone to deliver it to. And when I thought back, I couldn't remember when her last letter had arrived.

"A couple years later, after some other
155 things had happened, I made a trip back to the old neighborhood—something I'd never thought I'd do again. A Chicano family was living in our house. They told me they'd been there for quite a while. No, they didn't
160 know where the woman who sold them the house had moved to.

"I never did catch up with her, though I tried. I called around, asked the ladies at her church, even hired a detective for a
165 time. I thought of going up to her folks—not that I was sure where that was, but I could have found out. But I couldn't make myself. You know how certain childhood phobias can rule your life. So I persuaded myself they
170 wouldn't have known any more than I did."

Ah, Raven. I am wondering if you still search for her in all women, the lost mother. Forever beautiful, forever young.

"I needed to tell her so many things," says
175 Raven. "That I was sorry for my earlier coldness, that I understood, at least a little, why she'd left her home and denied who she was." He sighs. "I wanted to say, Let's try to forgive each other and start over...

180 "Things changed somehow when that letter was returned to me. Without my mother to show it to, my golden life seemed to lose some of its glitter." ■

3 Answer the questions, and discuss your answers in small groups.

a. What was Raven's relationship to his mother when he was in college? What was his relationship with her when he was telling his story? How do you know?

b. What cultural references does Raven make that Tilo, who didn't grow up in the United States, might not be familiar with?

4 **Vocabulary Check** Work with a partner. Use the context of the passage to determine possible meanings of the following expressions.

- **a.** strained (line 53)
- **b.** drivenness (line 63)
- **c.** recede (line 71)
- **d.** playing the market (line 87)
- **e.** gleaned (line 113)
- **f.** shard (line 123)
- **g.** made it (line 142)
- **h.** harsh (line 149)
- **i.** catch up with (line 162)
- **j.** glitter (line 183)

Think About It

5 Why do you think Raven told Tilo his story? Do you think Raven is satisfied with his life? Why or why not? Exchange ideas in small groups.

Write: Using Other People's Ideas

 Writing a formal research paper requires incorporating the ideas of others into your paper in order to introduce concepts, provide background and context, or support arguments. Whenever another person's ideas are used, credit must be given to the original author. Otherwise, you may be accused of **plagiarizing**.

The ideas of others are presented either directly, by quotation, or indirectly, by paraphrase. A direct quote uses the exact words of the original source. Short quotations must use quotation marks and are followed by a citation in parentheses. (Proper form for citations will be discussed in Unit 8.) Longer quotations (more than four lines) are single-spaced and done as an indented block of text. They also require citations. A paraphrase expresses the same ideas as the original but uses different words. Although the original author's wording is not used in paraphrasing, a citation is still required in cases where the paraphrase is presenting the original author's unique ideas.

6 Work with a partner. Read the examples on the next page and discuss their similarities and differences.

Source: Gardner, H. (1993). *Creating minds*. New York: Basic Books.

Short Quotation (author is mentioned before the quote)

In his book *Creating minds*, Howard Gardner (1993) describes how Martha Graham, after the death of her father, "felt free to chart her own future course" (p. 269).

Long Quotation (author is <u>not</u> mentioned before the quote)

The following describes the genesis of Martha Graham's artistic career:

Being inspired by a dance recital was one thing; making a career choice, quite another. The thought of their eldest daughter becoming a dancer hardly pleased the straightlaced Graham family. Parents and daughter settled on a compromise in which Martha would attend the Cumnock School, a junior college in which she could study liberal arts while pursuing her artistic interests. The relative freedom of the school pleased her. In 1914, when Graham was twenty, her father died of a heart attack. Graham now felt free to chart her own future course. (Gardner, 1993, p. 269)

What follows are the first steps of a great artist as she begins to make her way in the world. We see Graham establishing herself as a major force in the dance world, and...

Paraphrase (no page reference; author and date not mentioned)

As a teenager, Martha Graham wanted to become a dancer. However, her family was very conservative and thought that dance was not an acceptable career choice for people of their social class. Eventually they allowed Martha to attend the Cumnock School, a junior college where she could study dance along with a liberal arts curriculum. She enjoyed the school's relatively liberal atmosphere. Then, in 1914, the twenty-year-old Martha Graham took complete control of her own life following her father's fatal heart attack.

Martha Graham

Write About It

 7 Read the excerpt from *Creating minds,* by Howard Gardner, about the Russian composer Igor Stravinsky. Then write a paraphrase of the text.

> By his own testimony, Stravinsky was not a good student and usually performed at or below the average level for his class. Unlike Picasso, however, who appears to have had genuine learning problems, Stravinsky was simply uninterested in formal schooling and preferred throughout his life to educate himself. Ignoring his son's anti-scholastic inclinations, Stravinsky's father insisted that Igor follow in his footsteps and receive legal training. Stravinsky did not like law school at all, and this alienation only exacerbated his tense relation with his father and his general disaffection with his current situation (Gardner, 1993, p. 191).

_____

_____

_____

_____

_____

 8 **Check Your Writing** Exchange papers with a partner. Check your partner's paper for the accuracy of the paraphrase. Write your comments on the paper. When you get your paper back, revise it as necessary.

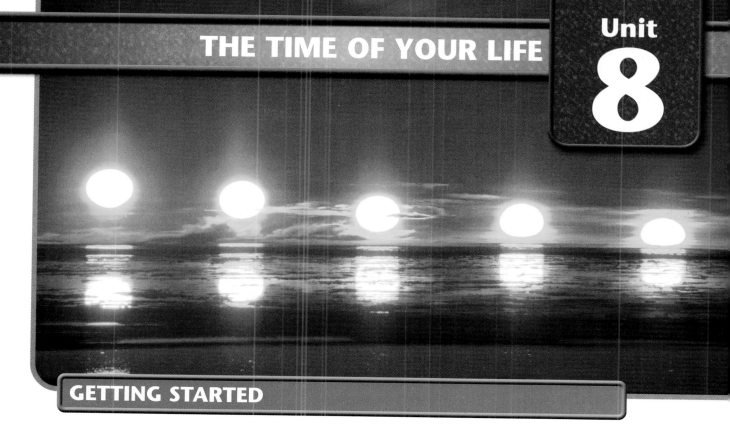

GETTING STARTED

Warm Up

All living organisms have internal biological clocks that control cyclic rhythms and related behavior. These clocks allow us to adapt to events in our environment.

1 Work with a partner. How does the time of day or night affect you? Are you a day or a night person? When do you function best?

 2 How much do you know about biological rhythms? Take the quiz and find out. Guess if the statements are **T** (true) or **F** (false) and circle your answers. Listen to check your answers and compare your score with a partner's.

1. A night person can become a morning person by working at it.   **T**   **F**
2. Heart attacks are most frequent at the end of a stressful day.   **T**   **F**
3. Driving while sleepy causes as many car accidents as driving while intoxicated.   **T**   **F**
4. Jet lag is "all in the mind." If you are disciplined, you won't get jet lag.   **T**   **F**
5. Most people need eight hours of sleep.   **T**   **F**
6. Blind people have more trouble sleeping than sighted people do.   **T**   **F**
7. Napping is only for babies and the elderly.   **T**   **F**
8. Teenagers who fall asleep in class should just go to bed earlier.   **T**   **F**
9. Breakfast is the most important meal.   **T**   **F**
10. A medicine that is safe at one time of day may harm you at another.   **T**   **F**

Figure It Out

Are there certain times of the day that you find yourself doing the same things or feeling the same way? Read the article and discover why.

Our societies have been built around obvious cycles: the daily rotation of the earth, the monthly revolution of the moon around the earth, and the yearly revolution of the earth around the sun. Isn't it more likely that biological cycles are caused by these geophysical events than by some internal clock?

5 　To find out, chronobiologists asked volunteers to live without the usual social and physical cues that we use to determine what time of the day or year it is. The volunteers lived without seeing the sun for the duration of the experiment. They didn't have contact with anyone
10 or anything that could give them clues about time— no current newspapers, radio, television, or regular appointments. In one study, the researchers worked irregular shifts, and male researchers were required to shave prior to meeting with the volunteers so that their
15 facial hair would not indicate time of day.

The volunteers' bodies were allowed to "freerun" so that the researchers could ascertain what would happen to biological cycles once the external cues had been eliminated. Several of the volunteers' physical traits, such as blood pressure and temperature, were monitored throughout the experiments. The volunteers tended to
20 establish a 25-hour day, sleeping about an hour later every day and keeping their internal clocks fairly constant.

Twenty-five hours? Why would our clocks be set at 25 hours? We seem to get up and go to bed on a 24-hour schedule, and our daily internal rhythms follow that time period, too. Chronobiologists have no clear answer to that question, but they
25 speculate about our having more flexibility to adapt to changes in seasonal day length with a 25-hour clock. External cues, especially sunlight, appear to reset the biological clock every day so that we don't drift into 25-hour days. Even though we might enjoy sleeping later and later, our social schedules and our alarm clocks won't let us.

Interestingly, animals that are active during the day tend to have circadian cycles that
30 are longer than 24 hours, while nocturnal animals tend to have cycles shorter than 24 hours. Chronobiologists have also studied ultradian cycles, such as heartbeat and respiration, as well as weekly, monthly, yearly, and longer cycles. How and why do all these cycles work together? Those are the questions that chronobiologists are asking.

  Vocabulary Check Work with a partner. Use the context of the reading to determine the meaning of the following words.

a. geophysical (line 4)　　　　**f.** reset (line 26)

b. chronobiologists (line 5)　　**g.** drift (line 27)

c. volunteers (line 8)　　　　　**h.** circadian (line 29)

d. shifts (line 13)　　　　　　　**i.** nocturnal (line 30)

e. ascertain (line 17)　　　　　**j.** ultradian (line 31)

Talk About It

 4 A chronobiologist is interviewing volunteers to determine their suitability for a study of biological cycles. Work with a partner. Take turns being the researcher and the volunteer and discuss the possible difficulties below. Use the conversation as a model.

Example: sleeping

ROLES	MODEL CONVERSATION	FUNCTIONS
Researcher:	Do you have trouble sleeping?	Ask about general problems.
Volunteer:	No. I'm usually able to sleep for eight hours without waking.	Answer the question and provide details.
Researcher:	Is it hard for you to wake up?	Ask a follow-up question.
Volunteer:	Not usually. But if I forget to set my alarm clock, I sometimes oversleep.	Respond and elaborate.

<u>Possible Difficulties</u>

a. getting along with others
b. cleaning up after yourself
c. changing your routine
d. going without sunlight
e. going without fresh air
f. (your own idea)

GRAMMAR

Gerunds and Infinitives

Gerunds and infinitives can both be used as subjects of sentences. Although the meaning is very similar, we usually use the gerund to suggest real actions and experiences, whereas we use the infinitive to imply a general, hypothetical meaning. We can avoid an infinitive subject by using *It* + *be* + infinitive.

> **Being a research subject** sounds interesting.
>
> **To do a six-month study** would be hard.
>
> **It** would be hard **to do a six-month study**.

Gerunds and infinitives often follow verbs. Some of these verbs take only gerunds; some take only infinitives; some can take either with minor differences in meaning. Finally, some can take either, but with a distinct difference in meaning.

Gerund only

Chronobiologists say that we should **avoid staying up** late on weekends.

Infinitive only

We should **decide to keep** our routines regular if we **want** our body clocks **to stay** constant.

Gerund and Infinitive (minor change in meaning)

I **like taking** afternoon naps on weekends. (I do it regularly.)
I **like to take** afternoon naps on weekends. (Hypothetically, I like it.)

Gerund or Infinitive (definite change in meaning)

She didn't **remember setting** the alarm clock. (. . . but it went off at the usual time.)
She didn't **remember to set** the alarm clock. (. . . so it didn't go off.)

In noun phrases that serve as objects, we use the **possessive + gerund** to emphasize the action rather than the agent.

I appreciate **your telling** me about sleep patterns. (I appreciate that you told me.)

Infinitives can have a subject which is often, but not always, preceded by *for*. With some verbs *for* is used, with others it is not used, and with yet others it is optional.

I hadn't intended **for you to spend** so much time on this study.

He convinced **me to learn** more about the field.

I'd like **(for) you to tell** me more.

A list of common verbs and expressions that are followed by a gerund or followed by an infinitive can be found on page 166.

1 Complete the passage by changing the verb in parentheses to a gerund or infinitive, as appropriate.

(1. Have) _____ a seven-day week seemed strange to sociologists since there was no corresponding geophysical event as there was with the solar day or the lunar month. They tended (2. attribute) _____ it to our cultures and not to biology.

However, other organisms also have a seven-day cycle, and a week is, after all, a quarter of a lunar cycle. At the end of the French Revolution, the revolutionary government wanted (3. establish) _____ a ten-day week, but the attempt failed (4. work) _____. In the former Soviet Union, the rulers also experimented with (5. modify) _____ the week by (6. try) _____ five-day and six-day weeks. Again, people rejected (7. change) _____ the length of their week. They seemed (8. need) _____ (9. have) _____ one day out of every seven in order to reset their body clocks.

Sometimes it is difficult (10. perceive) _____ our weekly rhythms, but these rhythms show up most strongly during times of stress. For the body (11. fight off) _____ a cold, it needs about a week. The symptoms of chicken pox show up about two weeks after the patient's (12. be) _____ exposed to the disease. Health care workers expect (13. see) _____ patients with pneumonia and malaria at greatest risk after one week of (14. fight) _____ these diseases. Transplant patients risk (15. have) _____ their bodies reject their new organs after seven days.

By (16. examine) _____ this evidence, sociologists have had reason to reconsider their previous ideas about the origin of the seven-day week.

☑ **2** **Check Your Understanding** On a separate sheet of paper, combine the sentences. Replace the word *something* in the first sentence with the words in the second sentence. Use a gerund or infinitive.

Example: Some cancer researchers are encouraging <u>something</u>.
Doctors give drugs at different times of the day.
Some cancer researchers are encouraging doctors to
give drugs at different times of the day.

a. They are reminding the doctors of <u>something</u>.
Normal cells have an approximate 24-hour cycle during which they grow and rest.

b. Researchers also expect <u>something</u>.
Cancer cells continue to grow while the normal cells are resting.

c. The fact that cells are more vulnerable to the effects of medication while they are growing allows <u>something</u>.
Doctors give their patients strong medications that fight the cancer cells but don't hurt the resting normal cells.

d. Under one system, doctors don't have to advise <u>something</u>.

Their patients take their medicines at certain times because the dosages are administered automatically.

e. The patients appreciate <u>something</u>.

The drugs have fewer side effects even though the medications might be very strong.

f. The doctors can convince <u>something</u>.

Their patients take these drugs for a longer period of time, too.

g. So far, patients are benefiting from this procedure, and doctors are hoping <u>something</u>.

Their patients continue to do well with this kind of treatment.

3 Work with a partner. Take turns asking and answering questions about SAD. Student A use the information in the chart below. Student B use the information in the chart on page 102.

Student A	
1. Question: Answer:	What is the meaning of "SAD"?
2. Question: Answer:	SAD symptoms: hard to wake up, overeating, difficulty concentrating; tired and depressed.
3. Question: Answer:	Treatment?
4. Question: Answer:	Another treatment: use an ionizer, a device that puts negative ions into the air. Negative ions lift mood. Another treatment: medication.

  4 **Express Yourself** Work with a partner. Describe how your personality and the activities you prefer to engage in change with the seasons. Share your information with another pair.

LISTENING and SPEAKING

Listen: A Guest Speaker

1 **Before You Listen** Work in small groups. Make a list of five questions that you would ask a chronobiologist. Discuss possible answers to your questions.

 Taking Question-and-Answer Notes When listening for understanding, efficient listeners often organize their notes along a question-and-answer format. One way to do this is to draw a vertical line dividing your paper into two columns—a narrower one on the left for the questions and a wider one on the right for the answers.

2 Listen to a question-and-answer session with a chronobiologist. As you listen, note the questions that were asked and their answers. Then compare your notes with a partner's.

3 Listen to the session again, and complete the missing information in the sentences below. Then compare your completed sentences and explain your choices.

a. According to Dr. Reid, people's individual body clocks _____.

b. Our bodies experience a natural slump _____.

c. As long as you eat something in the morning, it does not matter _____.

d. The best antidote to jet lag is _____.

e. People with Seasonal Affective Disorder, or SAD, generally _____.

Pronunciation

Sound-Spelling Dissimilarity (2)

The vowel sounds /aɪ/, /aʊ/, /eɪ/, /ɔi/, and /oʊ/ have a number of different spellings.

/aɪ/	/aʊ/	/eɪ/	/ɔi/	/oʊ/
line	now	hey	boy	go
my	crowd	late	noise	owe
die	count	wait	royal	home
sigh	ground	weigh	tabloid	coat

4 Predict the pronunciation of the vowel sounds, and put the words into the appropriate columns in the chart.

annoy	destroy	out	state
avoid	frown	own	straight
couch	hired	praise	thrown
craze	mind	sew	town
cry	noise	sight	zone

line /aɪ/	down /aʊ/	rain / eɪ/	boy /ɔi/	know /oʊ/

5 Listen to check your predictions.

 6 Work with a partner. Take turns reading the list of words, focusing on the sound-spelling link.

Speak Out

 Delivery Effective speakers know that *how* you say something is as important as *what* you say. Your body language says as much or more for you than your words. If you look and sound confident, you will make a better impression.

Delivery Tips

- Stand up straight with your shoulders back, but don't stand rigidly.

- Make eye contact. Don't stare at the floor, ceiling, or wall. Try to look at everyone in the audience; don't focus on one person or area.

- Speak loudly and strongly enough to be heard by everyone listening. Speak with confidence. You can vary the volume of your voice to add emphasis.

- Some gestures, such as indicating size or direction, can help your delivery. Avoid nervous gestures such as twisting a button or smoothing your hair.

- Pay attention to pacing. Don't speak too fast or too slowly.

- Rehearse your presentation so that you know how much time it will take.

Student B	
1. Question: Answer:	SAD = "Seasonal Affective Disorder." Affects people in the darker fall and winter months because their bodies aren't receiving enough light.
2. Question: Answer:	Symptoms of SAD?
3. Question: Answer:	Treatment = phototherapy—sitting in front of a bright light for thirty to sixty minutes a day.
4. Question: Answer:	Any other treatments available?

7 Work in small groups. Speak on one of the topics below for one minute. Focus on your posture, eye contact, volume, and other aspects of delivery.

> • the pros and cons of keeping a fixed schedule
>
> • the pros and cons of using medications to get over jet lag
>
> • the pros and cons of having early morning classes
>
> • (your own idea)

READING and WRITING

Read About It

 Before You Read How many hours of sleep each night do you need to feel your best in the morning? How many did (do) you average as a teenager? How do you react when you don't get enough sleep? Discuss with a partner.

STRATEGY **Reading for Credibility** When reading for critical analysis, it is important to question the credibility (believability) of the writer's claims and the sources that the author uses to support them. Ask yourself whether the information in the article sounds reasonable to you, or if these sources have sufficient experience or expertise to be trustworthy.

 Read the selection. As you read, note the explanations and the sources cited. Do you find them credible?

Why Teens Need More Snooze Time
by Shannon Brownlee

It's only 9:30 at night, but 15-year-old Ryan O. is already snuggling into bed, pulling a quilt decorated with dolphins and killer whales up over his ears. He tosses and turns for several minutes before drifting off—possibly because there are 12 electrodes fixed to his scalp and an infrared video
5 camera is recording his every move for researchers watching a video monitor in another room.

Ryan is one of several hundred teenagers who over the past decade have entered the twilight world of Brown University's Bradley Hospital sleep lab, allowing sleep physiologist Mary Carskadon to record their brain waves and
10 eye movements in slumber and to test how lack of sleep affects their mental and physical skills.

Carskadon's research has shown that teenagers who want to sleep all day are not lazy; they are simply following the dictates of their biological clocks.

(continued on next page)

Sleep is influenced by the circadian timing system, a bundle of neurons, embedded deep in the brain, that regulates production of a sleep-inducing chemical called melatonin and sets natural bedtime and rise time. Carskadon has shown that teenagers need more sleep than they did as children and that their biological clocks tell them to catch those extra winks in the morning. Most teens, she says, need nine hours and fifteen minutes of sleep a night, possibly because hormones that are critical to growth and sexual maturation are released mostly during slumber.

That means that the average teenager's brain isn't ready to wake up until eight or nine in the morning, well past the first bell at most high schools. When Carskadon and colleagues surveyed more than 3,000 Rhode Island high school students, they found that the majority were sleeping only about seven hours a night. More than a quarter of the students averaged six and a half hours or less on school nights. In another study, when students were asked to fall asleep in the lab during the day, many conked out within three or four minutes, a sure sign they were sleep-deprived. Carskadon also discovered that the students' melatonin levels were still elevated into the school day. "Their brains are telling them it's nighttime," she says, "and the rest of the world is saying it's time to go to school."

Kids who have to get up before their biological clocks have buzzed miss out on the phase of sleep that boosts memory and learning. Periodically during slumber, the brain enters rapid eye movement (REM) sleep, so called because the eyes dart back and forth under the lids. During REM sleep, the brain resets chemicals in the emotional centers and clears short-term memory banks, where the day's events are stored temporarily. Without enough REM sleep, Carskadon and others have discovered, people become cranky and depressed; their memory and judgment are impaired; and they perform poorly on tests of reaction time. Carskadon has found that teens who get the least sleep earn C's and D's, while those who get the most tend to get A's and B's.

One solution is to push back the time high schools start, something many schools are reluctant to do. Barring that, Carskadon and other experts say you should emphasize sleep's importance and help yourself get more through

55 biology: to encourage yourself to go to bed at a reasonable hour, keep the lights low in the evening, and open the curtains in the morning. Light absorbed through the eyes can reset the biological clock.

You can catch up on sleep on weekends—up to a point. Going to bed in the wee hours and snoozing until noon only disrupts the brain's clock further.
60 It's better to go to bed within about an hour of usual bedtime, and then sleep an hour or two later.

3 Discuss these questions in small groups.

a. What were the explanations for teens needing more sleep? Do you find these explanations believable? Why or why not?

b. What source does the author use to support her explanation? Do you think the source is trustworthy? Why do you feel this way?

c. What implied suggestion does the writer give to schools? What are some reasons you can think of for schools being reluctant to start later in the day?

4 **Vocabulary Check** Work with a partner. Use the context of the reading to determine the meaning of the following words.

a. snuggling (line 1)
b. quilt (line 2)
c. drifting off (line 3)
d. catch those extra winks (lines 18-19)
e. the first bell (line 26)

f. conked out (line 35)
g. boosts (line 42)
h. dart (line 44)
i. the wee hours (line 59)

Think About It

5 The article suggests that lack of sleep can lead to lower grades. What other problems can result from chronic lack of sleep?

Write: Creating a Bibliography and Gathering Information

 STRATEGY When doing research for an article or paper, it is important to take accurate notes. This information should include authors, dates, titles, volume numbers, places of publication, and names of publishers, according to APA style. It must be accurate, because it will be used to provide full documentation of your sources in a bibliography at the end of the paper. Page numbers are required in the bibiliography with direct quotations. However, page numbers should be placed in your notes in case you need to go back to the source material. You will also need them for in-text citations. (Note that titles of books and names of magazines are underlined when handwritten but should be italicized when done on a word processor.)

When the ideas or words of your sources are used in the text of the paper, the authors must be credited. This is done with citations in the text. These in-text citations differ depending on how the source is quoted or paraphrased.

Source: Campbell, J. (1986). Winston Churchill's afternoon nap. New York: Simon & Schuster.

Direct Quote: author not mentioned in sentence

"Biological clocks, timekeeping devices built into living organisms as part of their anatomy, are extremely ancient, being found in the most primitive species" (Campbell, 1986, p. 12).

Direct Quote: author mentioned in sentence

According to Campbell (1986), "Biological clocks, timekeeping devices built into living organisms as part of their anatomy, are extremely ancient, being found in the most primitive species" (p. 12).

Paraphrase: author not mentioned in sentence

Even the earliest species of plants and animals had internal clocks (Campbell, 1986).

Paraphrase: author mentioned in sentence

Campbell (1986) states that even the earliest species of plants and animals had internal clocks.

There are also required forms for citing works with more than one author.

- When the work cited has two authors, use both names and the date of publication: Perry & Dawson, 2000.

- When the work cited has two to five authors and is cited for the first time, use all names and the date of publication: Moore, Sulzman, & Fuller, 1999. After the first citation in the *same* paragraph, use the first author's name and *et al.* Moore et al. (**et al.** means "and others.") If the second citation of a work with two to five authors is in a different paragraph, use the first author's name and the date: Moore et al., 1999.

- When the work cited has six or more authors, for all citations (except if two are in the same paragraph) use the first author's name, et al., and the date: Samson et al., 1998. (If the work is cited twice in the same paragraph, the second citation does not have to include the date.)

Write About It

(6) Take notes as you research your topic. Make sure to include all the necessary citation information for each note. Bring your notes to class.

 (7) **Check Your Writing** Exchange notes with a partner. Check your partner's notes for content, clarity, and complete citation information. When you get your own notes back, add any missing information, based on your partner's comments.

GETTING STARTED

Warm Up

"Hot spots" are places where problems are likely to occur. In geology, a hot spot is where intensely hot liquid rock pushes up through the earth's surface, resulting in a volcano. More than 80 percent of the earth's surface is volcanic in origin.

1 Discuss the following questions in small groups.

   a. Are there any volcanoes in your country? When did they last erupt?

   b. Why do you think people live close to volcanoes, sometimes even building their homes on the slopes?

2 Listen to the description of the parts of the earth and of a volcano. Then use the words in the box to label the diagram.

ash	crust	gases
hot spot	magma	mantle

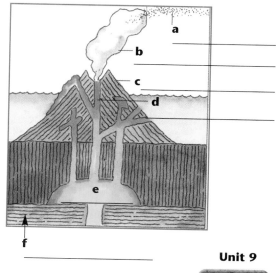

Figure It Out

Volcanoes have always been a source of fear and legend. Read how the Hawaiians explain their origin.

The folklore of the Hawaiian Islands includes a number of legends about the Fire Goddess, Pele. Although there are many versions of
5 the Pele stories, most of them agree that the Fire Goddess came from the South Seas with her younger sister and others in her family. When the travelers reached the Hawaiian
10 Islands, they settled on the northern island of Kauai. However, Pele's older sister, the Sea Goddess Nama Kasa, greatly disliked the beautiful, fiery young woman, so when Pele
15 tried to establish a home and light her magical fire on the island, the Sea Goddess sent water in the form of storms and tsunamis to put out the fire. Pele and her group moved
20 southward from island to island, always struggling against, and losing to, the Sea Goddess. Nevertheless, as she battled her older sister, Pele grew stronger and better able to defend
25 herself, until finally, on the Island of Hawaii, Pele established her flaming home in the crater of the volcano Kilauea. Here at last, the Goddesses fought to a draw, with neither able to
30 vanquish the other. To this day, Pele sends burning lava to her sister, and Nama Kasa cools the lava with water when it reaches the ocean. Moreover, sending lava from the volcano to the
35 ocean also makes Pele both the destroyer of the plants and animals that are in the path of the lava and the builder of the new land produced by the cooled lava.

40 As her title implies, the Fire Goddess is hot-headed and moody. It is she who determines when and where lava will flow, and it is she whom the villagers must appease so
45 as to keep the lava away from their homes. If you visit Kilauea, you may see food, flowers, and other gifts left at the edge of the volcano as offerings for Pele. If you are tempted
50 to pick up a rock as a souvenir of the mountain, think again, for another legend tells of jealous Pele pursuing those that steal her sacred stones and punishing them with fire until the
55 stones are returned. Indeed, every year hundreds of rocks are returned to Volcanoes National Park, where Kilauea is located, by chastened tourists who have felt the Fire
60 Goddess' fury.

Vocabulary Check Match the words on the left with their meanings on the right.

_____ **1.** folklore (line 1)

_____ **2.** settled (line 10)

_____ **3.** crater (line 27)

_____ **4.** fought to a draw (line 29)

_____ **5.** moody (line 41)

_____ **6.** fury (line 60)

a. ended a battle without establishing a winner

b. established a home

c. great anger

d. large depression in land

e. quick to change emotions

f. quick to smile

g. traditional stories

Talk About It

 A newspaper reporter is interviewing local residents about their experiences with natural phenomena. Work with a partner. Take turns asking and answering questions about a natural phenomenon. Use the conversation as a model.

Example: a wildfire

Roles	Model Conversation	Functions
Reporter:	Have you ever seen a volcanic eruption?	Ask about a natural phenomenon.
Resident:	I haven't seen a volcanic eruption, but I was once evacuated from my home because of a wildfire.	Describe an event.
Reporter:	Really? What happened?	Ask for information.
Resident:	When I was about ten, we didn't have much rain. The grass and trees were really dry, and they just caught fire.	Provide details.
Reporter:	Wow! So what happened then?	Encourage the speaker to continue.
Resident:	So, one day we saw these ugly, dark clouds building in the west. It looked like a thunderstorm was coming, but it turned out the hill was on fire.	Elaborate on the story.

Natural Phenomena

a. a hurricane

b. an earthquake

c. a tornado

d. a mudslide

e. an avalanche

f. (your own idea)

Word Order in Noun Phrases

A noun phrase consists of a noun and a number of other items that appear in a very specific order. Study the chart with different elements of a noun phrase.

Predeterminers	Determiners	Quantifiers	Intensifiers	Adjectives
all (of), both (of), half (of), most (of), every	a, an, his, my, our, that, the, these, this, those	few, a lot (of), one, two, etc., numerous, several	very, extremely, incredibly, rather, truly	Egyptian, green, hot, old, plastic, intricate, measuring, disappointing

Study the examples.

All the five *Hawaiian islands* are formed from volcanoes.

The two extremely intricate measuring *devices* failed to predict the volcanic activity.

Several rather disappointing *experiments* led to the closing of the volcanic measurement unit at the lab.

1 Create interesting noun phrases. Try to use words from all of the categories in the chart above.

_____

_____

_____

_____

_____

_____

Order of Adjectives

A noun phrase can have one or more adjectives. When more than one adjective occurs with a noun, the adjectives also occur in a specific order. Study the examples.

In Hawaii, we saw many **interesting small round black** pebbles on the beach.

We also visited some **fascinating molten red lava** flows.

The **ancient cool volcanic** ash in Oregon looks really different from the **flowing new hot** lava in Hawaii.

I really liked the **colorful red silk Polynesian** dress that our hostess wore.

Next year I want to see the **tall, conical Indonesian** volcanoes that I've heard so much about.

Maybe someday I'll be able to see an **exciting mushroom-shaped gray** cloud of steam coming from a **soon-to-erupt Alaskan** volcano.

---

2 Write these adjectives on the lines next to their categories. An example is given for each category.

used	damp	gigantic	lukewarm	fire-engine red
leather	Arabian	circular	new	beautiful
mysterious	molten	square	dark blue	huge
broken	metal	African	iron	old
tiny	important	purple	L-shaped	freezing
wooden	southern	modern	silk	remodeled

Age: *ancient,* _____

Color: *beige,* _____

Condition: *carved,* _____

Material: *cotton,* _____

Opinion: *attractive,* _____

Origin: *Turkish,* _____

Shape: *triangular,* _____

Size: *enormous,* _____

Temperature: *warm,* _____

3 Use the example sentences in the box to figure out the order that the adjective categories in Exercise 2 appear in. Then write the categories in their correct order on the lines below.

Order of adjectives

1. _opinion_   **4.** _____   **7.** _____

2. _size_   **5.** _____   **8.** _____

3. _____   **6.** _____   **9.** _____

4 **Check Your Understanding** Work with a partner. Unscramble these noun phrases, and write a sentence for each.

a. of one his	leather black old comfortable	jackets
b. my both of	white canvas old dirty	shoes
c. those both of	large red and blue Persian old	carpets
d. few a more	glass green small	bottles
e. of one several	antique enormous Hungarian	tables
f. of most the	carved well-known wooden	sculptures
g. the some of	expensive ceramic blue	dishes

1. _____ .

2. _____ .

3. _____ .

4. _____ .

5. _____ .

6. _____ .

7. _____ .

  5 **Express Yourself** On a separate piece of paper, write a paragraph describing a person, place, or thing, but do not state its name. Pay attention to the correct order of the adjectives. Read your paragraph to a partner, who will try to guess who or what you are describing.

LISTENING and SPEAKING

Listen: At a Party

 Before You Listen What are some possible threats that volcanic eruptions pose for people?

 Listening for Definitions
Conversations on scientific subjects may contain definitions of technical words. When listening for understanding, it is important to pay attention to cues that will tell you that the speaker is giving a definition.

2 Listen to a conversation between a retired vulcanologist and his granddaughter's friend. As you listen, write down the definitions of the words below. Compare your answers with a partner's.

a. pyroclastic flow _____ .

b. lahar _____ .

c. magma _____ .

d. lava _____ .

3 Listen to the conversation again and answer the questions. Compare your answers with a partner's.

a. How many people died in St. Pierre in the 1902 eruption in Martinique? What was responsible for their deaths?

b. How many people died in the 1883 eruption of Krakatau? What was responsible for most of their deaths?

c. What lessons can be learned from these incidents?

Pronunciation

Sentence Stress and Intonation in Thought Groups

English speakers group words together into logical phrases called **thought groups**. Each thought group has a combination of stressed and unstressed syllables, which creates a very distinct rhythm. At the end of a thought group, the speaker pauses briefly before continuing with the next thought group. The final thought group in a sentence carries sentence stress and sentence intonation.

Mount Etna in Sicily / erupted in 1669, / and this eruption / caused a local war.

4 Predict the division of the sentences into thought groups. Divide the sentences with slashes, as in the example above.

 a. There's a story that a lava war started when the citizens of the city of Catania were frightened because the lava from Mount Etna was flowing in the direction of their city.

 b. To avoid destruction, they began digging a ditch that would force the molten lava to flow in a different direction.

 c. Unfortunately, however, they redirected the lava flow toward the neighboring village of Paterno.

 d. As a result, the citizens of Paterno attacked the Catanians.

 e. The Catanians were defeated, and the lava flowed back on its normal course, eventually destroying half of the city of Catania.

5 Listen to the sentences to check your predictions.

6 Work with a partner. Take turns saying the sentences, paying attention to the division of the thought groups and the rhythm.

Speak Out

STRATEGY **Informative Talks: Explaining Steps of a Process** Informative talks are one common type of presentation. One kind of informative talk is one in which the speaker explains how something happens or is done. The process is presented in small steps using words such as *first*, *next*, and *finally* to clearly mark their order. Additionally, informative presentations often require specialized vocabulary that may need to be explained.

7 Work in small groups. Discuss the specialized vocabulary needed to explain these processes. Then speak for about one minute. Be sure to use words that help the audience understand the order of the steps in the process.

> • making a long-distance phone call
> • doing a search on the Internet
> • using a DVD player
> • preparing for a holiday or special occasion
> • burning a CD
> • (your own idea)

Read About It

1 **Before You Read** What do you know about the geologic process of island formation? Discuss this with a partner.

STRATEGY **Recognizing Literary Language** Literary works use a variety of language effects to create a mood, build a rhythm, and involve the reader in the world the writer is creating. When reading for personal interpretation and critical analysis, the reader can appreciate the full effect of the literary work by recognizing literary language.

Alliteration (words that begin with the same sound)

The **s**un **s**ank **s**lowly into the **s**mooth **s**ea.

Onomatopoeia (words that sound like the object they describe)

The sharp **snap** of the tree branch meant the tiger was approaching.

Repetition (using the same word repeatedly)

Dark, dark was the night, dully **dark**.

Hyperbole (exaggerating)

…more likely the roots of this future island were born in darkness and great waves and brooding nothingness.

---

2 Read the excerpt. As you read, circle examples in the text of the literary devices in the box and label them in the margin, using **A** for alliteration, **O** for onomatopoeia, and **R** for repetition.

"From the Boundless Deep"
an excerpt from *Hawaii*
by James Michener

Millions upon millions of years before man had risen upon earth, the central areas of this tremendous ocean were empty, and where famous islands now exist, nothing rose above the rolling waves. Of course, crude forms of life sometimes moved through the deep, but for the most part the central ocean
5   was marked only by enormous waves that arose at the command of moon and wind. Dark, dark, they swept the surface of the empty sea, falling only upon themselves, terrible and puissant and lonely.

Upward, upward, for nearly four miles they climbed, those agitated bubbles of air, until at last upon the surface of the sea they broke loose and formed a
10   cloud. In that instant, the ocean signaled that a new island was building. In time it might grow to become an infinitesimal speck of land that would mark the

(continued on next page)

great central void. No human beings then existed to celebrate the event. Perhaps some weird and vanished flying thing spied the escaping steam and swooped down to inspect it; more likely the roots of this future island were born
15 in darkness and great waves and brooding nothingness.

For nearly forty million years, an extent of time so vast that it is meaningless, only the ocean knew that an island was building in its bosom, for no land had yet appeared above the surface of the sea. For nearly forty million years, from that extensive rupture in the ocean floor, small amounts of liquid rock seeped
20 out, each forcing its way up through what had escaped before, each contributing some small portion to the accumulation that was building on the floor of the sea. Sometimes a thousand years, or ten thousand, would silently pass before any new eruption of material would take place. At other times gigantic pressures would accumulate beneath the rupture and with
25 unimaginable violence rush through the existing apertures, throwing clouds of steam miles above the surface of the ocean. Waves would be generated which would circle the globe and crash upon themselves as they collided twelve thousand miles away. Such an explosion, indescribable in its fury, might in the end raise the height of the subocean island a foot.

30 But for the most part, the slow constant seepage of molten rock was not violently dramatic. Layer upon layer of the earth's vital core would creep out, hiss horribly at the cold sea water, and then slide down the sides of the little mountains that were forming. Building was most sure when the liquid rock did not explode into minute ashy fragments, but cascaded viscously down the sides
35 of the mountains, for this bound together what had gone before, and established a base for what was to come.

How long ago this building took place, how infinitely long ago! For nearly forty million years the first island struggled in the bosom of the sea endeavoring to be born as observable land. For nearly forty million submerged
40 years its subterranean volcano hissed and coughed and belched and spewed forth rock, but it remained nevertheless hidden beneath the dark waters of the restless sea, to whom it was an insignificant irritation, a small climbing pretentious thing of no consequence.

And then one day, at the northwest corner of the subocean rupture, an
45 eruption of liquid rock occurred that was different from any others that had preceded. It threw forth the same kind of rock, with the same violence, and through the same vents in the earth's core. But this time what was thrown forth reached the surface of the sea. There was a tremendous explosion as the liquid rock struck water and air together. Clouds of steam rose miles into the air. Ash
50 fell hissing upon the heaving waves. Detonations shattered the air for a moment, and then echoed away in the immensity of the empty wastes.

But rock had at last been deposited above the surface of the sea. An island—visible were there but eyes to see, tangible were there but fingers to feel—had risen from the deep.

55   This was the restless surge of the universe, the violence of birth, the cold tearing away of death; and yet how promising was this interplay of forces as an island struggled to be born, vanishing in agony, then soaring aloft in triumph.

60 You men who will come later to inhabit these islands, remember the agony of arrival, the rising and the fall, the nothingness of the sea when storms throw down the rock, the triumph of the mountain when new rocks are lifted aloft.

3 Michener's only references to people are in the first and last paragraphs. However, he sometimes refers to inanimate objects as if they had human motivations. This technque is called **personification**. Work with a partner. How many examples of personification can you find in the excerpt?

 4 **Vocabulary Check** Match the words on the left with their meanings on the right. Use the context to help you.

    _____ **1.** infinitesimal (line 11)   **a.** openings

    _____ **2.** apertures (line 25)   **b.** very small

    _____ **3.** minute (line 34)   **c.** explosions

    _____ **4.** viscously (line 34)   **d.** microscopic, extremely small

    _____ **5.** detonations (line 50)   **e.** touchable

    _____ **6.** tangible (line 53)   **f.** rush, flow

                                          g. thickly, stickily

Think About It

5 What mood is Michener trying to create with his use of language effects? Is he successful in this? Why or why not? Discuss with a partner.

Write: Writing the Research Paper

 In the body of the paper, support paragraphs present and develop the argument presented in the thesis statement. Each support paragraph has its own topic, which is presented and developed through a topic sentence and additional sentences of explanation, definition, or comparison, as well as through the use of examples and citations. Each support paragraph ends with a transitional sentence that links the current paragraph with the following paragraph.

Write About It

6 Review the idea map and outline that you created in Unit 6. Compare the outline with the notes you took in Unit 8. Organize your notes according to the outline. Remember that each section of your outline must support your thesis.

7 Prepare an idea map, outline, and notes on one of the topics below.

- the process of the formation of a volcano
- the process of how other natural disasters, such as earthquakes or hurricanes, develop
- the steps you should take to protect yourself in case you are in a natural disaster
- (your own idea)

  8 **Check Your Writing** Exchange your work with a partner. Comment on your partner's work. When your work is returned to you, revise as necessary.

GRAMMAR

IDENTIFYING UNNECESSARY WORDS This type of question tests your ability to recognize common errors made by adding unnecessary articles, pronouns, prepositions, or making incorrect comparisons. Not every sentence in this section contains a mistake. When you see these words, always check their context to be sure that they belong in the sentence.

A Decide which sentences are correct and which have an incorrect additional word. Circle the incorrect word. Write C on the line for correct sentences.

_____ **1.** Human circadian rhythms make (for) working night shifts or rotating shifts very difficult to adjust to.

_____ **2.** Research into this problem has resulted in some more practical suggestions that are recommended for any company with a night shift.

_____ **3.** First, they suggest that weight rooms be installed because exercise boosts alertness and helps night workers sleep better during the daytime.

_____ **4.** Companies are also urged to offer a nighttime childcare for workers' children.

_____ **5.** Because sugar and fats are more harder to digest at night, companies should provide snacks of fruits and vegetables.

_____ **6.** Napping is encouraged for nighttime workers as 30 minute naps help workers feel refreshed.

_____ **7.** Using light which simulates sunlight is a worthwhile investment because it will keep workers for feeling upbeat and alert.

USING MNEMONICS: Successful students often use an invented word, a poem, or a sentence as a mnemonic (memory) device to help them remember important rules. For example, OCSMOSACT could help someone remember the correct order for different categories of adjectives: *Origin, Color, Size, Material, Opinion, Shape, Age, Condition,* and *Temperature.*

B Each sentence has four underlined words or phrases. Circle the letter of the word or phrase that is incorrect.

1. <u>It is vital</u> that parents <u>recognize</u> the <u>strong extremely influence</u> they   A B ©D
        A   B   C
have on their <u>children's</u> educational decisions and career paths.
            D

2. <u>The most significant</u> factors appear <u>being</u> the size of the family,   A B C D
           A   B
<u>parenting</u> style, and the <u>attitudes</u> parents have about work in general.
   C   D

3. <u>It be essential</u> that parents <u>recognize</u> that the <u>long, ever-changing process</u>   A B C D
       A   B   C
of career choice <u>begins</u> when children are still young.
        D

4. Educators are concerned about <u>parents</u> <u>not being aware of</u> the importance   **A B C D**
                                   A   **B**

   of their <u>positive or negative enduring</u> influence <u>on their children</u>
                         C   **D**

   in this way.

5. <u>It is important</u> that <u>parents of young</u> <u>impressionable</u> pre-schoolers   **A B C D**
         A   **B**   **C**

   <u>are made aware of this influence</u>.
           D

6. Educators <u>ask</u> that this advice <u>be not held off</u> until high   **A B C D**
              A   **B**

   school because <u>ignoring</u> the importance of the pre-school years <u>is</u>
                   C   **D**

   short-sighted and harmful.

7. There are <u>various practical</u> suggestions <u>of what</u> parents should   **A B C D**
                   A   **B**

   not <u>put off</u> <u>to do</u> to help their children's career development.
        C   **D**

8. Parents need <u>stress</u> the importance of values such as <u>being</u> punctual,   **A B C D**
             A   **B**

   responsible, and <u>respectful</u>, and the importance of always <u>doing your best</u>.
                  C   **D**

> **STRATEGY** ▶ **OPEN DIALOGUE** This task demonstrates your ability to complete gaps in a short conversation. Some standardized tests target specific grammatical points for gap-filling. Because the correct answers depend on the context, always read the complete conversation to understand the main ideas before filling in missing words.

C **Complete the dialogue with your own words. Be sure to read the complete conversation before filling in the gaps.**

A: What could Bill do to find out if he really wants to be a doctor?
B: I think that volunteering at a clinic **(1.)** _____.
A: How long would he need to volunteer to see if being a doctor is something he'd like?
B: It's hard to say exactly. I guess I'd recommend **(2.)** _____.
A: That's quite a long time. I think not having an income for a whole month will be hard on him.
B: Yes, it'll be difficult but it's better than making the wrong decision.
A: **(3.)** _____?
B: Full time? No, I don't think so. They'll probably just need to know in advance how much time he's able to give them.

VOCABULARY

WORD FORMATION These questions test your ability to use different forms of words. One type of word formation exercise asks you to form a new part of speech (noun, adjective, adverb, etc.) by combining the stem word with a suffix. Decide on the part of speech you need, then check your spelling. For example, decide if the word ends in –ence or –ance, -able or -ible, -sion or -tion.

A Use one of the following suffixes and the stem words in parentheses to form a word that will fit the sentence grammatically.

-ness	-asion	-al	-simal	-ed	-able	-ture	-lore	-ible	-ation

1. There is a lot of (folk) _folklore_ about natural disasters, some of which is true and some of which is not.

2. Changes in climate and geophysical events can cause (natur) _____ disasters such as avalanches and tsunamis.

3. There can be more than one (aper) _____ in a volcano crater and they can vary greatly in size.

4. The tension in the air before a natural disaster such as an earthquake or volcano eruption can seem almost (tang) _____ as evidenced by unusual animal behavior.

5. Scientists compile a lot of data and (inform)_____ from many different sources to make reasonable predictions.

6. Many of the people who have made a significant contribution in their field have shared the characteristic of (driven) _____.

7. Sometimes information that seems (infinite) _____ in importance when compiled together with other information becomes significant.

STRATEGY ▶
COLLOCATIONS Collocations are words that often appear together. Some tests may ask you to display your skill with collocations in order to determine if you understand the differences in how words are used.

B Find the word or phrase in the box that best completes the passage below.

hours of the morning	an ambition	a knack for	after herself
off to sleep	an open mind	up on	into a career change
the company	a lot of		

      Tomorrow morning, Marie would start her new job. She had been **(1.)**_____ to make some changes in her life for a long time. She hadn't been prepared to jump **(2.)** _____ until she'd investigated all the options, but she was finally ready. Marie had been nursing **(3.)**_____ to be the boss. She finally found a job where she could run **(4.)** _____ and do things her way. In her new job, a lot of changes needed to be made, but Marie had **(5.)** _____ reorganizing. For the first few weeks she would listen to the employees' complaints about their former boss. It would be necessary to keep **(6.)** _____ and reserve judgment. She knew this would take time and that she'd probably be working into the wee **(7.)** _____ in the weeks to come. But once she'd made changes, she would be able to catch **(8.)** _____ needed sleep. She made herself think about something else so she could drift **(9.)** _____. Finally, she conked out and slept until her alarm clock jolted her out of her dreams.

WRITING

STRATEGY ▶
  ANSWERING ESSAY QUESTIONS When taking a standardized test, you won't have access to any original texts, so direct quotes won't be possible. You can, however, paraphrase, expressing the original ideas of an author, but in your own words. You will have to give a citation, where the paraphrase is presenting the author's original unique ideas.

Write an essay in response to one of the questions below. Allow yourself no more than thirty minutes. Include at least one paraphrase of another person's ideas.

A. How do you think becoming more knowledgeable about chronobiology and circadian rhythms can help us in our daily lives?

B. At what age or stage in school do you think children or young adults should receive career counseling?

C. Do you think it is possible that we will be able to be better prepared in the future to withstand natural disasters? If so, how?

GETTING STARTED

Warm Up

1 People travel for many reasons: business, pleasure, education, and family. What are some of the difficulties of modern-day travel? What are some of the benefits?

2 Which of these statements do you agree with? Which do you disagree with? Write **A** (agree) or **D** (disagree). Compare your answers with a partner's.

_____ **a.** You need a lot of money to travel comfortably.

_____ **b.** You need to be young and carefree to travel.

_____ **c.** The single, most important ingredient of successful travel is a positive attitude.

_____ **d.** You aren't truly educated until you've traveled abroad.

_____ **e.** To travel you need to be able to expect the unexpected.

_____ **f.** You can learn a lot about your own country by traveling abroad.

_____ **g.** Your best side emerges when you travel.

_____ **h.** Air travel has lost its glamour.

_____ **i.** Traveling is the best way to meet new people.

 3 Now listen to an interview with a travel journalist. Does she agree with your opinions? Discuss with a partner.

Figure It Out

How prepared are you for the surprises that travel can offer? Read about one woman's painful discovery that she should learn to listen to advice.

"Be prepared," my friends all said when I set out to conquer Europe. "Be sure to reserve hotel rooms, check train schedules, and make lists of things to see, so that when you get home you'll have seen all the important landmarks." And they were right. But I didn't listen. As a

5 result, I can go on for hours about where you end up when you take the wrong train from Sitges to Barcelona, but I can't tell you about my impressions of Gaudi's Sagrada Familia Cathedral because I never got there. Instead I was stuck for three hours at the end of some little local train line, and if I hadn't met a friendly shopkeeper with a car, I might

10 have spent the night there on the platform.

"Be prepared," they said. "Pack light but carry a big suitcase. By the time you head home you'll have been accumulating gifts and souvenirs for weeks, and you'll need some way to lug all that stuff back." And they were right. But I didn't listen. A little tote bag was all I took, and

15 that was stuffed to overflowing before I even started. Sure enough, after a few days of carting around a growing assortment of shopping bags, I finally broke down and bought another suitcase. A big one. At least I didn't have to worry about how to carry *that* home.

"Be prepared," they said. "Bring
20 sturdy, comfortable shoes. You'll have covered hundreds of miles on foot by the time this trip is over, and you don't want sore feet to cramp your style." And they were
25 right. But I didn't listen. I thought that my flip-flops were all that I needed. I ended up hobbling down the Champs-Elysées with blisters and one bare foot after an altercation with
30 an aggressive poodle with a taste for rubber.

"Be prepared," they said. But I didn't listen. I wasn't prepared, and I paid the price. But I don't really mind. The one thing they didn't tell me was, "By the time you take your next trip, you'll have gotten so much mileage out of your wild stories from the last one that you'll

35 probably go off unprepared again." They didn't tell me that, but if they had, they would have been right. And thankfully, by the time you decide to travel again, you'll have long forgotten all that wasn't wonderful and exciting. You'll be anxiously awaiting the new adventures.

Vocabulary Check Work with a partner. Use the context to determine the meaning of these words and expressions from the reading.

a. go on for hours (line 5)
b. lug (line 13)
c. carting around (line 16)
d. broke down (line 17)
e. flip-flops (line 26)
f. hobbling (line 27)
g. paid the price (line 32)
h. gotten so much mileage out of (lines 33-34)

Talk About It

 Two friends are talking about future goals and dreams. Work with a partner. Take turns asking and answering about goals and dreams for the future. Use the conversation as a model.

Example: sail to the South Pacific

ROLES	MODEL CONVERSATION	FUNCTIONS
Wishful Friend:	Before I'm too old, I'd like to buy my own sailboat and sail it to the South Pacific.	State a dream or aspiration.
Skeptical Friend:	And just when do you think you'll do that?	Show skepticism.
Wishful Friend:	By the time I'm thirty-five, I'll have saved enough to buy the boat. After that, there's no hurry. I hope to reach Tahiti by the time I'm forty. Think of it! By then I'll have been sailing the seas, free as a bird, for five years!	Explain how you will realize your dream and live your life.

Goals and Dreams

a. go around the world by bicycle
b. climb the tallest mountains on each continent
c. explore the Amazon
d. get a black belt in a martial art
e. write a book
f. shop the souks and bazaars of the Middle East.
g. (your own idea)

GRAMMAR

Future Perfect Tense and the Future Perfect Progressive

The future perfect allows us to look back from some point in the future. It is often used with time expressions like *by next Wednesday, by this time (tomorrow, next week, etc.), by the time (something happens)*. To form the future perfect, we use *will/be going to + have + past participle*.

The future perfect progressive refers to an action or state that is still in progress in the future, but was started at an earlier time in the future.

The future perfect progressive is also often used with the same time expressions as the future perfect. To form the future perfect progressive, we use *will/be going to + have been* + present participle.

Future Perfect

(point in the future)   (completed action)

<u>By this time next month</u>, we **will have left** for Brazil.
Before I arrive, I'**ll have** already **sent** you a number of letters.

Future Perfect Progressive

(future action in progress for a while)   (point in the future)

We **will have been traveling** for twelve months by <u>this time next year</u>.

---

1 A counselor is advising students who have chosen a study-abroad program. Circle the answer which best complete the sentences.

Congratulations! You've decided to study abroad. Let's think ahead a little bit. When you return from your year abroad, you **(1. will spend/will have spent)** a year in a different culture. I guarantee that, by this time next year, everyone here **(2. will go through/will have gone through)** some form of culture shock. It usually happens like this: Soon after arriving, most of you **(3. are going to experience/are going to have experienced)** a honeymoon phase in which everything is new, different, and exciting. After a few weeks, as the novelty wears off, you might **(4. be experiencing/have been experiencing)** some anxiety, but you eventually **(5. will work out/will have worked out)** most of your problems. Ideally, by the time you're ready to come home, you **(6. will make/will have been making)** the most of your experience abroad and forgetting that you were ever uneasy.

2 Complete the paragraph with the appropriate form of the verb in parentheses. Compare your answers with a partner's.

The full "shock" of culture shock **(1. hit)** _____ for certain after you find yourself irritated, or even angry, with how the new culture does things. By the end of this phase, some people probably **(2. give up)** _____ and they **(3. go)** _____ home. I expect that a couple of months from now, a few of you **(4. decide)** _____ that studying abroad is just not for you at this time. However, if you make it through the period of irritability and anger, you'll find that you **(5. start)** _____ to cope with the new culture and can even get around fairly well. You **(6. adapt)** _____ since your first day in the new country, and you may discover that you go through these phases at different rates: sometimes quickly, sometimes slowly, and sometimes more than once. Eventually, if all goes well, you **(7. reach)** _____ the point where you feel comfortable in both cultures.

3 Work with a partner. Write a short travel brochure describing the benefits of visiting your country or home region. Include information about sights visitors will have seen, special dishes they will have eaten, activities they will have engaged in, and the sort of people they will have met by their return. Share your information with a partner.

Sentence Fragments

All sentences in English consist of a subject and a predicate (verbs or verb phrases, and sometimes a complement). A sentence fragment is a group of words that is punctuated like a sentence but does not have both a subject and a verb and does not express a complete thought. A subordinate clause punctuated as a sentence is also a fragment, because it does not express a complete thought.

Sentence Fragments	Corrected Sentences
1. Tourism brought many negative results. A destroyed coastline.	1. Tourism brought many negative results, such as a destroyed coastline.
2. He paid the taxi driver. Even though he shouldn't have.	2. He paid the taxi driver even though he shouldn't have.

 4 Correct the sentence fragments in the paragraph.

After you return home from a trip, especially a long one. You are not necessarily finished with culture shock. You may experience another kind of shock. Called return, or reverse, culture shock. If you have adapted to a new culture, you will have to readapt to your home culture. You may see your home with "new eyes." Because you have changed. Just as you adjusted to the new culture, you will readjust to your home culture. Be patient with yourself.

Run-on Sentences

A simple sentence expresses one complete thought and contains one subject and one predicate. When two or more complete thoughts are improperly joined, the result is called a run-on sentence and is to be avoided.

Run-on Sentence	Corrected Sentence
1. Tourism brought about positive and negative changes in several societies, one example of a positive change is the increase in jobs in the service industry.	1. Tourism brought about positive and negative changes in several societies. One example of a positive change is the increase in jobs in the service industry.
2. Tourism prompted the construction of numerous resorts, it also destroyed the coastline.	2. Tourism prompted the construction of numerous resorts; it also destroyed the coastline.

5 Correct the run-on sentences in the paragraph.

> "Ethnocentrism" is the practice of accepting our own cultural values as the only correct ones, it is very easy to judge other cultures by our culture's standards as we only really know the culture in which we were born. Travelers need to guard against ethnocentrism if they don't, they won't take full advantage of the benefits of travel. Having an open mind, even when traveling in different parts of your own country, will help you appreciate the rich variety of cultures, you may also learn about yourself and your own culture.

6 Exchange your travel brochure from Exercise 3 with a partner. Check your partner's papers for sentence fragments and run-on sentences. Correct the errors.

"I understand that in your country this thing is done quite differently."

7 **Check Your Understanding** Check the future forms you are *most likely* to use in these situations.

	Simple Future	Future Perfect	Future Perfect Progressive
a. Talking about your future achievements in your new culture			
b. Describing your future home and how long you've lived there			
c. Preparing a list of items you predict will not be available in your new country			
d. Planning your future job opportunities			

8 **Express Yourself** Imagine you can read the future for your partner. Use the simple future, future perfect, and future perfect progressive to make predictions of things to come in his or her future. State your predictions to your partner, and see if these predictions seem accurate or plausible to him or her.

LISTENING and SPEAKING

Listen: An Overseas Haircut

1 **Before You Listen** Who usually cuts your hair? What problems can people have when they get their hair cut? What additional problems might someone have when getting a haircut overseas or by someone who doesn't speak his or her language? Discuss with a partner.

 STRATEGY **Listening for Details** When listening for personal interpretation, effective listeners focus on details such as shapes, sounds, feelings, or moods. By doing this, they can more clearly picture in their minds the events, places, and people a speaker is describing.

 2 Listen to the speaker tell a story about getting a haircut. As you listen, take notes on the details the speaker describes. What kind of mood does he create? Discuss with a partner.

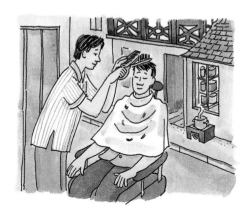

3 Listen to the story again and answer the questions. Discuss your answers with a partner.

   a. What were the cultural problems?

   b. How were they resolved?

   c. Was this story interesting to you? Why or why not?

Pronunciation

Using Stress-Timing and Linking

A thought group has one or more stressed syllables. Between these stressed syllables are one or more unstressed syllables. Stressed syllables occur at regular intervals in English. To accomplish this, we pronounce the unstressed syllables more quickly.

a	**good**	**trip**
a **real**ly	**good**	**trip**
an in**cred**ibly	**fun**	**trip**
an over**whelm**ingly	ex**cit**ing	**trip**

When we express a thought in quick, connected speech, we do not pause after saying each word—we link the words together. To do this, we often drop sounds from the beginning and/or the end of certain words. For example, the /**h**/ is often dropped in function words and pronouns. Also, words are often reduced and attached to other words.

Some words that can be linked in connected speech:

he	him	Just as h̸e is.
her	them	I saw h̸er in Mexico.
his	you	I like h̸is hats. Do you like ṯhem?

---

4 Predict the pronunciation. Underline the stressed syllables. Cross out the letters of any sounds that will be dropped.

   Example: I <u>like</u> h̸er.

   A: José Antonio went to Chile.

   B: Why did he go to Chile?

   A: He went for his cousin's wedding.

   B: I didn't know he had a cousin in Chile. Where does he live?

   A: *She.* I think her home is just outside Santiago.

🎧 **5** Listen to check your predictions.

6 Work with a partner. Take turns pronouncing the sentences on page 129, focusing on stress-timing and linking.

Speak Out

In meetings and discussions, a group is often trying to make a decision or solve a problem. However, some members may have personal reasons for slowing or stopping the discussion. For example, a person may disagree with the ideas or want his or her own ideas accepted. This person may also joke or refuse to cooperate.

STRATEGY ➤ **Using and Dealing with Communication-Blocking Tactics**
Satisfying individual needs is important; however, groups must also accomplish as much as possible during meetings. When a group member blocks progress, the whole discussion may be jeopardized.

> **A:** . . . as you can see, my solution is really the only credible one.
>
> **B:** We'll consider it, but let's hear from Leslie now.
>
> **A:** Oh, this is just a waste of time. Do we really have to hear all the other solutions?
>
> **B:** Yes, we have to get input from everyone. Now, let's hear from Leslie.

7 Put an **X** next to the expressions that might be used to block progress in a group discussion.

_____ **a.** I don't know why you're discussing this. I'm never going to agree to this plan.

_____ **b.** Sandra, what do you think about this?

_____ **c.** Now, that's a dumb idea.

_____ **d.** You people never listen to me.

_____ **e.** Lena, could you tell us more about that?

_____ **f.** I'm sorry; I didn't hear you. Could you repeat that?

_____ **g.** Did you hear the joke about . . .

8 Work in small groups. Discuss one of the topics from the list. One member of the group should take on the role of blocker. The others should try to continue to make progress. At the end of the discussion, talk about how the group could further discourage the blocker's behavior.

> • You're in charge of setting up entertainment for a class party.
>
> • You must decide on where to hold next year's graduation ceremony.
>
> • You must decide on what incentive to give to your students.
>
> • (your own idea)

Read About It

 Before You Read What was your first experience of going far away from home? Was it a scary experience? Why or why not?

STRATEGY **Recognizing Descriptive Language** When reading for personal interpretation, effective readers focus on the descriptive language the writer uses. Writers use descriptive language not only to give the reader a physical sense of people, places, and things, but also to create a particular mood and reinforce main ideas.

2 Read the excerpt. As you read, circle any descriptive passages that you find particularly effective.

The Enigma of Arrival
by V.S. Naipaul

Indeed, there had been a journey long before—the journey that had seeded all the others, and had indirectly fed that fantasy of the classical world. There had been a journey, and a ship.

This journey began some days before my eighteenth
5 birthday, in late July, 1950. It was the journey that for a year I had feared I would never be allowed to make. So that even before the journey, I lived with anxiety about it.

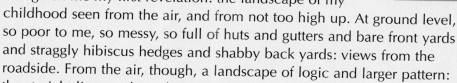

There had, first, been an airplane—a small one of the period, narrow, with a narrow aisle, and flying low. This
10 had given me my first revelation: the landscape of my childhood seen from the air, and from not too high up. At ground level, so poor to me, so messy, so full of huts and gutters and bare front yards and straggly hibiscus hedges and shabby back yards: views from the roadside. From the air, though, a landscape of logic and larger pattern:
15 the straight lines and regularity and woven, carpetlike texture of sugarcane fields, so extensive from up there, leaving so little room for people, except at the very edges; the large, unknown area of swampland, curiously still, the clumps of mangrove and brilliant-green swamp trees casting black shadows on the milky-green water; the
20 forested peaks and dips and valleys of the mountain range. A landscape of clear pattern and contours, absorbing all the roadside messiness: a pattern of dark green and dark brown, like camouflage, like a landscape in a book, like the landscape of a real country. So that at the moment of takeoff, almost—the moment of departure—the landscape of my
25 childhood was like something I had missed, something I had never seen.

(continued on next page)

Minutes later, the sea. It was wrinkled, as in the fragment of the poem by Tennyson. It glinted in the sun; it was gray and silver rather than blue; and, again as in the fragment by Tennyson, it did

30   crawl. And then the little airplane rose just above the clouds and flew like that, just above the clouds, until we reached Puerto Rico. From someone who had travelled to Jamaica, perhaps in an even smaller airplane, five years before, I

35   had heard about the beauty of the clouds seen

from the top. So this was a beauty and an experience that I was ready for, and was overwhelmed by. Always, above the cloud, the sun! So solid the cloud, and pure. I could only look and look; truly to possess that beauty, to feel that one had come to the end of that particular

40   experience, was impossible. To see what so few men had seen! Always there, the thing seen, the world above the clouds, even when unperceived; up there (as down below, sometimes, at sunset) one's mind could travel back—and forward—aeons.

For eight hours—or was it thirteen?—we drove on in a dark sky to New

45   York. Hours away from the life of my island, where nothing had savor, and even the light had a life-killing quality (as I thought), I lived—like any peasant coming for the first time to a capital city—in a world of marvels.

I had always known that this world existed, but to find it available to me for only the price of a fare was nonetheless staggering. With the marvels,

50   however, there went, as in a fairy story, a feeling of menace. As the little plane droned and droned through the night, the idea of New York became frightening. Not the city so much as the moment of arrival: I couldn't visualize that moment. It was the first traveller's panic I had experienced.

I wrote in my diary. I had bought, for that purpose, a cheap little lined

55   pad with a front cover that held envelopes in a pocket. I also had an "indelible" mauve pencil, of the sort that serious people in Trinidad—especially officials—used in those days. When you licked the pencil, the color became bright; dry, the color was dull. I had bought the pad and the pencil because I was travelling to become a writer, and I had to start.

60   My memories of my arrival late at night in New York are vague. I think back hard now, and certain details become clearer: a very bright building, dazzling lights, a little crowd in a small place, a woman official with a very sharp "American" accent calling out the names of certain passengers.

There was a letter for me. A man from the British Consulate should

65   have met me. But the plane had been delayed, so he had gone home, leaving this letter, which gave me only the name of the hotel he had booked me into. He should have protected me. He left me at the mercy of the taxi-driver who took me into the city. The driver cheated me,

charged too much; and then, seeing how easily I acquiesced, he stripped
70 me of the few remaining dollars I had on me (I had a few more, a very
few, hidden in my suitcase) by claiming them as a tip. I felt this
humiliation so keenly that memory blurred it soon, and then eradicated
it for many years.

The shower was in my own room: a luxury. I had dreaded having
75 to use a communal one. One tap was marked "Hot." Such a refinement
I had never seen before. In Trinidad, in our great heat, we had always
bathed or showered in water of normal temperature, the water of the
tap. A hot shower! I was expecting something tepid, like the warm
bathwater (in buckets) that my mother prepared for me (mixed with
80 aromatic and medicinal leaves) on certain important days. The hot water
of the Hotel Wellington shower wasn't like that. Hot was hot. Barely
avoiding a scalding, I ducked out of the shower cubicle.

So the great day ended. And then—it was my special gift, and
remained so for nearly twenty years, helping me through many crises—
85 I fell asleep as soon as I got into bed, and didn't wake up again until
I had slept out all my sleep.

3 Choose one of the descriptive passages that you circled in Exercise 2.
Work with a partner and discuss the way in which Naipaul uses
description to create a mood or support an idea.

4 Work with a partner. Discuss the questions and share your answers
with the class.

a. What does the title "The Enigma of Arrival" refer to?

b. How does Naipaul compare his childhood memories of his village
in Trinidad? How do those memories compare with the view he
saw from the plane? How did that make him feel?

c. What language does Naipaul use to describe the following items
in this excerpt: *the airplane, fields, swampland, the mountain range,
the sky over New York City, the hotel shower*?

5 **Vocabulary Check** Match the words on the left with their
meanings on the right. Use the context of the reading to help you.

_____ **1.** revelation (line 10)   **a.** small, close-together groups

_____ **2.** landscape (line 10)   **b.** wonders, incredible things

_____ **3.** texture (line 15)   **c.** make a reservation

_____ **4.** clumps (line 18)   **d.** an area of countryside or land

_____ **5.** marvels (line 47)   **e.** insight, sudden awareness

_____ **6.** booked (line 67)   **f.** claim

                                          g. surface roughness or smoothness

Think About It

 In referring to his first impression of New York City, Naipaul states, "I lived—like any peasant coming for the first time to a capital city—in a world of marvels." What were your feelings the first time you left home? What were the circumstances? Did the reality match your expectations?

Write: The Introduction

The introduction of an article, essay, or short research paper provides the reader with information necessary to understand the writer's perspective on the topic. It explains the reason for the paper and in the thesis statement describes the purpose of the paper.

 The writer must take his or her audience into consideration, as this affects the way in which the introduction is developed. If the audience is the general reader, the introduction will contain an overview and explain any specialized terms or concepts that might be unfamiliar. If the audience is well informed about the topic, the introduction will contain more specialized, sophisticated material.

 Reread "Implants in the Brain" on page 66 and answer the questions. Discuss your answers in small groups.

- How did the writer control the flow of the introductory paragraph?

- Did the sentences move from more general to more specific or from more specific to more general?

- Where in the paragraph is the thesis statement? Do you think this is the most effective place for it?

- What audience did the writer of "Implants in the Brain" have in mind?

Write About It

 Take a sample of your own writing from previous units and review the introduction. Revise it again using what you have learned about effective introductions.

  Check Your Writing Exchange introductions with a partner. Give written feedback on your partner's paper. When you get your own paper back, revise as necessary.

GETTING STARTED

Warm Up

Cooperation and competition are part of the life around us. Trees in a forest compete for more sun. As a result, they all try to grow to be the tallest. Lions cooperate to hunt down food and to protect their young. We all cooperate and compete in some respect.

1 Which of the following statements do you agree with? Which do you disagree with? Why? Discuss your ideas with a partner.

_____ **a.** The best competitors always win, in sports and in life.

_____ **b.** In learning, cooperation is more important than competition.

_____ **c.** All a team needs is one superstar who can do everything.

_____ **d.** Games based on cooperation rather than competition are boring.

_____ **e.** Competition is the best motivator.

2 Both competition and cooperation are part of our lives. With a partner, discuss how competition and cooperation play roles in different situations.

3 Listen to a description of the Lakota tribe's view of teamwork. How is it described? Is your culture's concept of teamwork similar or different? Discuss with a partner.

Figure It Out

Do you come from an "I" culture or a "we" culture? Read the excerpt on the next page to find out.

Researchers have recently begun to look at the notion that certain cultures—including the majority white culture in the United States—represent "I" cultures, societies that prize the individual over the group. Other cultures tend to be "we" cultures, where connectedness, cooperation, and collaboration are more the
5 rule. While consulting with the Bureau of Indian Affairs (BIA) in South Dakota a few years ago, I learned an interesting lesson about "we" versus "I" cultures. A few years before, a large sum of money had been invested by the Bureau in a handicrafts business that was to be taken over, in stages, by the members of the reservation. When the business failed, some observers chalked it up to
10 "lack of Indian initiative." A talk with an insider, however, revealed a very different story. It turned out that the BIA had imposed a business model based on the values of the white American "I" culture: rewarding individual performance through incentive programs, encouraging competition between individuals, and engaging in other "I"–related activities. Lakota society—being a
15 "we" culture—doesn't think primarily in terms of personal rewards and achievements. The guiding principle is more often "we all move together, cooperatively, or none of us move at all." So when the native Americans failed to move up the corporate ladder as single individuals, their actions were misinterpreted as lack of motivation.

20   "We" cultures tend to make up the greater part of the world's population, including many African, Middle Eastern, Asian, and Latin American societies. Two researchers studying management
25 systems in Kenya, Africa, noted: "In Kenyan tribes nobody is an isolated individual. Rather, his or her uniqueness is a secondary fact… First, and foremost, he or she is several people's contemporary… In this system, group activities are
30 dominant, responsibility is shared and accountability is collective." In Arab cultures individuals are known by their *nisba*—or group identification (e.g., Umar Al-Budhadiwi = Umar of the Buhadu Tribe). Similarly, Japanese workers, like the native Americans described above, are embarrassed to be singled out for praise but strive for excellence within a group context. Americans are taught, at a very
35 early age, to embrace competition and cooperation. Take a spelling bee in school. Each team vigorously competes against the other, whereas members of a team cooperate. Good players on a team are given a place of esteem. Bad players are considered a liability. What is the hidden message behind games of competition and cooperation?

4 **Vocabulary Check** Work with a partner. Use the context to determine the meanings of the following words and expressions.

a. taken over (line 8)
b. chalked it up to (line 9)
c. initiative (line 10)
d. incentive (line 13)
e. move up the corporate ladder (line 18)

f. contemporary (line 29)
g. accountability (line 30)
h. singled out (line 33)
i. strive (line 34)

Talk About It

 5 A worker and his supervisor are discussing working conditions in their company. Work with a partner. Take turns being the different workers and discuss your responses to the working conditions. Use the conversation as a model.

Example: Everyone in your company gets the same bonus.

ROLES	MODEL CONVERSATION	FUNCTIONS
Supervisor:	I don't think it's fair for everyone to get the same bonus. People who do more deserve more.	Complain about a policy.
Worker:	You seem to think either the executives or the supervisors deserve more, but a business needs all kinds of jobs.	Counter the argument.
Supervisor:	Yes, but workers who have more responsibility should be entitled to more rewards.	Support your argument.
Worker:	I understand what you're saying, but all workers have responsibilities. The whole group of employees is more motivated if everyone shares in the profits equally.	Challenge the supporting information.

Working Conditions

a. The top salesperson gets a bonus; everyone else gets nothing.
b. Workers with children receive special benefits; single workers don't.
c. Managers get full health care benefits; workers get only limited benefits.
d. The most recent hire will be the first person fired.
e. (your own idea)

GRAMMAR

Irregular Nouns

Some nouns have irregular singular and plural forms that influence subject-verb agreement. For example, some nouns are plural in form but take singular verb forms.

> **Athletics <u>consists</u>** of both competition and cooperation.
>
> **One hundred dollars <u>is</u>** the entry fee for that competition.
>
> | Academic Subjects | Diseases | Units of Measure | Others |
> |---|---|---|---|
> | economics | measles | two hours | politics |
> | linguistics | mumps | ten dollars | news |
> | physics | shingles | thirty meters | headquarters |

Some nouns take plural verb forms but are singular in meaning.

> His **pants <u>were</u>** made especially for this magic show. (only one pair of pants)
>
> The city **outskirts <u>were</u>** the setting for his performance. (only one outskirts)
>
> | Clothes/Apparel | Tools | Abstract Nouns |
> |---|---|---|
> | glasses | scissors | riches |
> | shorts | pliers | thanks |
> | pajamas | tweezers | surroundings |

Some nouns have the same form for both the singular and plural, but meaning can change.

> **French <u>is</u>** spoken in some parts of Canada. (the language)
>
> The **French <u>are</u>** proud of their culture. (the people)
>
> | Chinese | series | species | deer | fish |

In American English, collective nouns sometimes take singular verb forms, and sometimes plural verb forms.

> My **family <u>is</u>** bigger than most families.
>
> The **police <u>are</u>** keeping order at the outdoor concert.
>
> **Collective Nouns That Are Singular and Plural**
>
> | class (is) | team (is) | audience (is) |
> | classes (are) | teams (are) | audiences (are) |
>
> **Collective Nouns Taken as Plural**
>
> | people (are) | police (have) | cattle (go) |

1 Complete the sentences by circling the correct forms of the verbs in parentheses.

The Lakota people **(1. lives/live)** in the north central part of the United States. These Native Americans **(2. has/have)** been compared with National Basketball Association (NBA) players: Both groups **(3. has/have)** to work together in order to achieve their goals. The Lakota **(4. was/were)** known for traveling long distances to confront enemies, not for the riches that **(5. was/were)** often acquired but for the experience of working together. One hundred miles **(6. was/were)** not an exceptional distance for them to travel on foot or horseback.

Likewise, an NBA team **(7. travels/travel)** long distances to confront other teams. While a series of individual moves **(8. is/are)** often impressive, the only statistics that really **(9. matters/matter) (10. is/are)** the ones that give the score at the end of the game. Higher mathematics **(11. is/are)** not necessary to determine the winners. The news of a victory **(12. precedes/precede)** the "warriors," and their audience **(13. cheers/cheer)** them accordingly.

Countability

Nouns can be either countable or non-countable, depending on the context they are used in. When the noun is a concept or abstract idea, it is often a non-count noun. When it shows one example or instance of the concept, it is a count noun.

> **Business is** a competitive field. (non-count noun)
> A **business** with a lot of competition **has** to work to be successful. (count noun)
> **Basketball is** my favorite sport. (non-count noun)
> There **are** two **basketballs** in the hallway. (count noun)

Some nouns change their meanings when they are used as non-count nouns.

> **a game** (count noun): entertainment or sport
> **game** (non-count noun): animals hunted for food
>
> **a play** (count noun): a theater performance
> **play** (non-count noun): amusement

2 Complete the passage below using the appropriate form of the noun in parentheses.

In New Games, we emphasize **(1. challenge)** _____ rather than **(2. competition)** _____. We also believe that the **(3. challenge)** _____ of any **(4. game)** _____ should be meaningful to all the players, so that the players remain the focus of the game. Many New Games require traditional sports **(5. skill)** _____ such as **(6. speed)** _____, **(7. strength)** _____, **(8. coordination)** _____, and quick **(9. reflex)** _____. But these games might also be won with **(10. brainpower)** _____, through **(11. strategy)** _____. And there are other games that demand a **(12. sense)** _____ of humor.

3 **Check Your Understanding** What would you say in these situations? Read the situation. Then, create a response using an appropriate form of the word in parentheses. Compare your answers with a partner's.

a. You want your teacher to advise you on courses to take. (advice)
You ask: Can you _____?

b. You are at a job interview and are discussing your previous employment. (experience)
You say: I have _____.

c. You're at the airport and need to find a hotel. (accommodation)
You ask: Where _____?

d. Your car was in a traffic accident and you're discussing the repairs with a mechanic. (damage)
You ask: What _____?

Express Yourself Work with a partner. Choose one of the situations above and create a dialogue. Then perform your dialogue for another pair.

LISTENING and SPEAKING

Listen: A Business Class

1 **Before You Listen** Think of three different kinds of businesses. How do employees cooperate in these kinds of businesses? How do they compete?

Listening for Explicit and Implicit Assumptions

Most scientific and social theories are based on certain assumptions. When listening for critical analysis, it is important to pay attention to both the explicit and implicit assumptions that ideas and opinions are based on.

 2 Listen to a discussion in the business class. As you listen, take notes and answer the questions.

    a. What are the explicit assumptions that the professor bases her discussion on?

    b. What argument is used to challenge one of these assumptions?

    c. How does the professor defend her assumptions?

3 Listen to the discussion again. What are some of the implicit assumptions that the discussion is built on? Compare your ideas with a partner's.

Pronunciation

Blending and Linking Words in Connected Speech

When we produce words in a thought group, we link them together. The last sound of one word often affects the pronunciation of the first sound of the next. When we link words, sounds are sometimes added, deleted, or changed.

Sound Deletion

Tell him	/tɛlɪm/	(/h/ is deleted)
The first three	/ðəfɚðri/	(/t/ is deleted)
Recent quakes	/risənkweiks/	(/t/ is deleted)

Sound Addition

Two apples	/tuwæplz/	w is added between vowels
Three others	/θriyʌðɚz/	y is added between vowels

Sound Change

Where did you go? /wɛrdʒugo/ (/d/ and /y/ become /dʒ/)

 4 Predict the sound deletions, additions, or changes in the boldfaced words below. Write **D** (deletion), **A** (addition), or **C** (change) on each line.

_____ **1.** Take out **what you** take in.

_____ **2.** **Plenty of people** know this motto of hikers and campers.

_____ **3.** If **we observe** this rule, everyone will be able to enjoy cleaner recreation areas.

_____ **4.** But some hikers leave empty bottles on the trail simply to get **rid of them**.

_____ **5.** Unfortunately, the rest of us have to deal **with their** trash.

_____ **6.** Why do social **factors seem** to motivate some of us but not others?

_____ **7.** It seems that you **need your** own internal motivation; social pressure alone isn't enough.

_____ **8. When nobody** cares about consequences, everybody suffers.

5 Listen to check your predictions.

6 Work with a partner. Take turns saying the sentences, focusing on sound deletions, additions, and changes.

Speak Out

STRATEGY **Giving a Persuasive Talk** In class, in business, and in social situations, it is sometimes necessary to persuade others to change their beliefs, opinions, or behavior. You may want to use information and narrative to support your ideas, but your main task is to produce a change in your listeners. A persuasive talk contains the same elements as other presentations, though there are some special considerations.

Guidelines for Persuasive Talks

a. Open your presentation with shared experiences, problems, or goals. If you present yourself as a reasonable person with an understanding of your listeners, they will be more likely to respond well to your request for change.

b. Ask for a small change. Asking for a complete change may be asking too much.

c. Acknowledge any arguments that people who don't agree with you might have. Then tell why your position is stronger.

d. End your presentation by reminding your listeners why change is needed.

---

7 Match the guidelines in the box with their examples below.

_____ **1.** I'm sure that we've all had the experience of...

_____ **2.** Some people may say that sports build character, but there are other, less hurtful, ways to build character.

_____ **3.** Although we can't eliminate competition completely, we can reduce it in our personal lives.

_____ **4.** I won't try to convince you that gray is more elegant than black is, but I will try to show you why gray is a better choice for our school uniforms.

_____ **5.** Going for a walk every other day may not sound like much, but it can be the first steps toward a healthier mind and body.

8 Choose a topic from the list and develop it into a 4-5 minute talk. Then give your presentation to a small group.

> • Let children play, not compete.
> • Competition brings out the best in people.
> • There is too much competition in schools.
> • (your own idea)

Read About It

Before You Read Did you play team sports when you were younger? How did the experience affect you later in life?

STRATEGY **Evaluating an Argument** Efficient readers do not automatically accept or reject an argument. When reading for critical analysis, they evaluate how effective the author has been in supporting his or her argument and decide if these are valid reasons for accepting or rejecting the author's assertions.

Read the selection. As you read, pay attention to how the author supports the argument. Is the argument convincing or unconvincing?

Get Up a Game
by Steve Chandler

When Michael Jordan, one of the best basketball players ever, was a sophomore in high school, he was *cut* from his high school basketball team. Michael Jordan was told by his coach that he wasn't good enough to play high school basketball. It was a crushing disappointment for a young
5   boy whose heart was set on making the team, but he used the incident— not to get mad, not to get even, but to get better.

We no longer value heroes and individual achievement as we once did. "Competition" has become a bad word. But competition, if confronted enthusiastically, can be the greatest self-motivating experience in the world.

10   What some people fear in the idea of competition, I suppose, is that we will become obsessed with succeeding at somebody else's expense. That we'll take too much pleasure in defeating and therefore "being better" than somebody else. Many times during conversations with my children's teachers, I am told how the school has progressively removed grades
15   and awards from some activities "so that the kids don't feel they have to compare themselves to each other." They are proud of how they've softened their educational programs so that there's less stress and competition. But what they are doing is not softening the program— they are softening the children.

20   If you are interested in self-motivation, self-creation, and being the best you can be, there is nothing *better* than competition. It teaches you the valuable lesson that no matter how good you are, there is always

(continued on next page)

somebody better than you are. That's the lesson in humility you need, the lesson those teachers are misguidedly trying to teach by removing grades.

It teaches you that by trying to beat somebody else, you reach for more inside of yourself. Trying to beat somebody else simply puts the "game" back into life. If it's done optimistically, it gives energy to both competitors. It teaches sportsmanship. And it gives you a benchmark for measuring your own growth.

The poet William Butler Yeats used to be amused at how many definitions people came up with for happiness. But happiness wasn't any of the things people said it was, insisted Yeats. "Happiness is just one thing," he said. "Growth. We are happy when we are growing."

A good competitor will cause you to grow. He will stretch you beyond your former skill level. If you want to get good at chess, play against somebody better at chess than you are. In the movie *Searching for Bobby Fisher*, we see the negative effects of resisting competition on a young chess genius until he starts to *use* the competition to grow. Once he stops taking it personally and seriously, the game itself becomes energizing. Once he embraces the intriguing fun of competition, he gets better and better as a player, and grows as a person.

I mentioned earlier that I'd heard a report on the radio that there was a Little League (children's baseball) organization somewhere in Pennsylvania that had decided not to keep score in its games anymore because losing might damage the players' self-esteem. They had it all wrong: Losing teaches kids to *grow* in the face of defeat. It also teaches them that losing isn't the same as dying, or being worthless. It's just the other side of winning. If we teach children to fear competition because of the possibility of losing, then we actually *lower* their self-esteem.

Compete wherever you can. But always compete in the spirit of fun, knowing that finally surpassing someone else is far less important than surpassing yourself.

If you're better at a game than I am, when I play against you and try to beat you, it's really not you I'm after. Who I'm really beating is *the old me*. Because the old me couldn't beat you.

3 Identify examples in the reading that illustrate the elements below, and write their line numbers next to each.

_____ **a.** thesis

_____ **b.** acknowledgement of the opposing point of view

_____ **c.** suggestion or call to action

_____ **d.** quotation

_____ **e.** personal anecdote

_____ **f.** anecdote about someone else

4 Do you accept the author's claims? Why or why not? Refer to specific portions of the text.

☑ **5** **Vocabulary Check** Choose the appropriate meaning for each word or expression as it was used in the article.

_____ **1.** cut (line 2)	**a.** dismissed	**b.** wounded
_____ **2.** heart was set on (line 5)	**a.** was emotional about	**b.** strongly desired
_____ **3.** get even (line 6)	**a.** seek revenge	**b.** become level
_____ **4.** beat (line 26)	**a.** hit	**b.** win against
_____ **5.** benchmark (line 29)	**a.** point of reference	**b.** line on a chair
_____ **6.** after (line 60)	**a.** at a later point in time	**b.** competing with

Think About It

6 Discuss the following questions in a small group.

a. Think of a time when you lost at something. What did you learn? Would you have learned as much if you had won instead? Why or why not?

b. Do you think the author was writing for an "I" culture or a "we" culture? What makes you think that?

Write: Writing the Concluding Paragraph

 STRATEGY The conclusion of the work is writers' last chance to persuade their readers of their opinions. Generally, the conclusion ties all the threads together by summarizing how the supporting material has made the case. In addition, just as in the mental process of "reaching a conclusion," the conclusion of a piece of writing should suggest some kind of "next step," based on the assumption that the thesis has now been well-argued. Writers may make judgments, suggest courses of action, give warnings, or pose new questions for further inquiry. As a matter of style, it is also common to close with a memorable line or two.

7 Reread "Implants in the Brain" on page 66. Look at the last few paragraphs. What lines restate the writer's thesis? What "next step" does the writer suggest? What is the memorable closing? Do you find it to be effective? Discuss with a partner.

Write About It

8 Write a rough draft of the conclusion of a paper, paying special attention to a "next step" and memorable closing.

_____

_____

_____

_____

_____

_____

_____

  Check Your Writing Exchange conclusions with a partner. Use the questions below to give feedback on your partner's work. When you get your own paper back, revise it as necessary.

- Is there a restatement of the thesis?
- Has the "next step" been included?
- Does the paper end with a memorable conclusion?

GETTING STARTED

THE FAR SIDE   By GARY LARSON

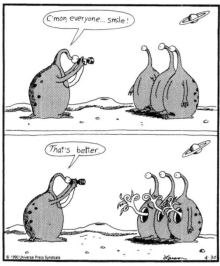

THE FAR SIDE © 1990 Universal Press Syndicate.
Reprinted with permission. All rights reserved.

THE FAR SIDE   By GARY LARSON

THE FAR SIDE cartoon by Gary Larson is reprinted by
permission of Chronicle Features, San Francisco, CA.

Warm Up

There are many reasons why people laugh. Some people are good at making witty remarks while others enjoy telling jokes or making puns. Still others like to do silly things or to play practical jokes. Most theorists agree that inconsistency or incongruity plays an important role in laughter. That is to say, when we expect a situation to end one way but it ends in a totally unexpected way, we often laugh.

1. How do you express humor? Are there any ways that you do not like to see humor expressed? Discuss with a partner.

2. Look at the cartoons. What role does incongruity (inappropriate or unexpected behavior for the situation) play in these situations? Discuss with a partner.

 3. Work with a partner. Listen to the joke. What role does incongruity play in the story?

Figure It Out

There's an old saying, "Laughter is the best medicine." Find out why that is so.

Dr. William Fry, a Stanford professor of psychiatry, has studied laughter. In his research, he has found that a five-year-old child laughs more than four hundred times a day. But adults' rates of laughter shrivel to fourteen times daily—or less.

5 In recent years, other researchers' studies have shown that laughter has a number of positive effects on the body:

- The body's temperature rises, making an individual feel warmer.
- Blood pressure drops.
10 - People's muscles contract, then relax, as they laugh.
- Breathing becomes deeper.
- Serum oxygen levels are elevated, which benefits the cardiovascular system, heightens energy levels, and reduces tension.

15 Laughter also boosts the immune system. It activates T lymphocytes and natural killer cells, both of which help destroy invading microorganisms. In addition, laughter increases the production of immunity-boosting gamma interferon and speeds up the production of new immune cells. And it reduces levels
20 of the stress hormone cortisol, which can weaken the immune system. It appears that when we laugh, we release endorphins, which are natural painkillers.

A robust laugh gives many of the organs of our bodies a good workout. Dr. Fry has discovered that laughing for ten minutes
25 is similar to rowing one hundred strokes on a rowing machine. A person's muscles tighten and relax, thereby growing stronger. Thanks to a pulmonary cardiac reflex, a person's pulse can double from, say, 60 to 120. Laughing is aerobic; laughing with gusto lets our bodies perform an internal massage.

☑ ④ **Vocabulary Check** Match the words on the left with their meanings on the right.

_____ **1.** shrivel (line 4)   **a.** chemicals that make us feel better
_____ **2.** serum (line 12)   **b.** increasing oxygen levels in the body
_____ **3.** boosts (line 15)   **c.** for instance
_____ **4.** immune (line 15)   **d.** action of moving a boat through water
_____ **5.** endorphins (line 21)   **e.** increases
_____ **6.** rowing (line 25)   **f.** fighting against disease or infection
_____ **7.** aerobic (line 28)   **g.** related to blood
                                       h. get smaller

Talk About It

 5 A comedy team is performing a routine. Work with a partner. Take turns being the joke teller and the "straight man," using the cues below. Use the conversation as a model.

Example: a pun

ROLES	MODEL CONVERSATION	FUNCTIONS
Joke Teller:	Why is six afraid of seven?	Set up the joke or story.
"Straight Man":	I don't know. Why?	Prompt the joke teller.
Joke Teller:	Because seven eight (ate) nine.	Finish the joke.
"Straight Man":	I don't get it.	Respond to the joke.
Joke Teller:	You know—"eight" and "ate"? Oh, forget it.	Follow up on the response.

Routines

a. another pun

b. a knock-knock joke

c. a story about an embarrassing incident

d. something amusing that a child said

e. a joke from another language, translated into English

f. (your own idea)

GRAMMAR

Possession: 's and *of*

In English, we add an apostrophe and the letter *s* or just an apostrophe to a noun to express possession (*A has* **B** or **B** *belongs to A*).

Who Owns It	What Is Owned	Meaning
Bryson	Bryson**'s** book	Bryson has a book.
		or Bryson wrote a book.
the doctor	the doctor**'s** car	The doctor has a car.
the doctors	the doctor**s'** cars	The doctors have cars.
my boss	my boss**'s**/boss**'** desk	My boss has a desk.
my bosses	my bosse**s'** desks	My bosses have desks.
Agnes	Agnes**'s**/Agnes**'** job	Agnes has a job.
children	children**'s** toys	The children have toys.
Emi	Emi**'s** story	Emi told/wrote a story.
		or There is a story about Emi.

We can also use the possessive **'s** for certain time expressions.

| a day's work | a week's vacation | a month's salary |

1 Complete these rules for forming possessives by adding the correct possessive form.

    a. With most singular nouns, we use _____.
    b. With singular nouns ending in *s*, we use _____ or _____.
    c. With regular plural nouns, we use _____.
    d. With irregular plural nouns, we use _____.
    e. With plural nouns ending in *s*, we use _____.

Possession can also be expressed using *of* (trunk *of* the car). We usually use *of* when the possessor is not a person.

the hood **of** the car	The car has a hood.
the opening **of** the theater	The theater opened.
the source **of** inspiration	Inspiration comes from a source.
the medium **of** television	Television is a medium.

2 Combine the nouns in each item to make possessives, paying attention to word order.

    a. the rest/my life
    b. witty sayings/Oscar Wilde
    c. each other/stories
    d. the bottom/the sea
    e. managers/ability

    f. secret/success
    g. senses of humor/my friends
    h. Thomas/funny stories
    i. children/games
    j. comedy/the history

3 Complete the sentences with the appropriate form of the possessive.

Dorothy Parker **(1.)** _____ witty quips illustrate her famous sense **(2.)** _____ humor. Once, for example, after seeing one of Katharine Hepburn **(3.)** _____ performances, she commented, "She ran the whole gamut **(4.)** _____ emotions from A to B."

Another person known for sharp wit was England **(5.)** _____ Winston Churchill. Although Churchill **(6.)** _____ wisecracks often bordered on rudeness, they are still appreciated to this day. Once Nancy Astor, a member **(7.)** _____ the British Parliament, was upset with one **(8.)** _____ the prime minister **(9.)** _____ decisions and told him, "Winston, if I were married to you, I'd put poison in your coffee." Churchill replied to Astor **(10.)** _____ remark by saying, "Nancy, if you were my wife, I'd drink it."

4 On a separate piece of paper, rewrite the passage using an appropriate expression of possession for each item in parentheses.

(1. the Ford car company + founder), Henry Ford, didn't tolerate inefficiency well. He would go to **(2. the executives + offices)** rather than having them come to his office when he wanted to meet with them. He said, "I go to them to save time. I've found that I can leave **(3. the other fellow + office)** a lot quicker than I can get him to leave mine."

Abraham Lincoln, **(4. the United States + sixteenth president)**, was also impatient with **(5. his subordinates + inefficiency)**. Toward **(6. 1862 + end)**, Lincoln was unhappy with General George McClellan, **(7. the U.S. army + leader)**, who wasn't attacking the Confederate army in the U.S. Civil War. At this stage of the war, the **(8. numbers + advantage)** belonged to the U.S. army. **(9. Lincoln + letter)** to McClellan was brief: "If you don't want to use the army, I should like to borrow it for a while. Yours respectfully, A. Lincoln."

Parallel Structures

In written English, we use parallel grammatical structures in a sentence to express ideas of equal importance. For example, if we use an adjective form for one of the ideas, we should use it for the others as well. Sentences that don't use parallel structures for ideas of equal importance can be awkward and confusing.

Nonparallel Structures	Parallel Structures
1. He preferred **listening to jokes** to **puns**.	1. He preferred **listening to jokes** to **listening to puns**.
2. He preferred **the comedy clubs in the city** to **small towns**.	2. He preferred the comedy clubs in **the city** to **those in small towns**.

 5 Rewrite the sentences on a separate sheet of paper using parallel structures. Compare your sentences with a partner's. Did you find different ways to make the structures parallel?

a. Charles Darwin noticed that smiles were the one facial expression recognized in both the Eastern Hemisphere and the West.

b. An effective way to combat sickness is to laugh regularly, or failing that, smiling a lot.

c. Smiling regularly reduces your heart rate and the blood pressure too.

d. Some hospitals have now set up laughter rooms, so patients can watch comic videos or reading humorous books to improve their health.

 6 **Express Yourself** Work with a partner. Take turns telling each other short, humorous stories. Share your best stories with another pair.

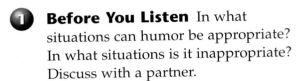

LISTENING and SPEAKING

Listen: A Business Seminar

1 **Before You Listen** In what situations can humor be appropriate? In what situations is it inappropriate? Discuss with a partner.

STRATEGY ▶ **Listening for Supporting Details**
When listening for critical analysis, an effective listener pays attention to the support that a speaker gives for his or her argument. If the support is weak or difficult to follow, the listener can sometimes ask for elaboration or clarification.

🎧 **2** Listen to a talk on productivity in the workplace. As you listen, take notes on the details the speaker uses to support her idea that productivity is related to humor. Give an example of each of the types of humor the speaker mentions. Compare your answers with a partner's.

3 Listen to the talk again. What information would you like the speaker to clarify or elaborate on? Write a question that you could ask the speaker during the question-and-answer period.

Pronunciation

Shift of Sound and Stress in Word Families			
There are sometimes changes in vowel and consonant sounds from one member of a word family to another. Stress can also shift from one syllable to another.			
Verb	**Noun**	**Adjective**	**Adverb**
pro**duce**	pro**duc**tion	pro**duc**tive	pro**duc**tively
in**clude**	in**clu**sion	in**clu**sive	in**clu**sively
Noun	**Noun (agent)**	**Adjective**	**Adverb**
soci**o**logy	soci**o**logist	socio**log**ical	socio**log**ically
e**con**omy	e**con**omist	eco**nom**ical	eco**nom**ically

Predict where the stress will be in each word by underlining the syllables with the strongest stress.

a. bibliography   bibliographical   bibliographically
b. pharmacology   pharmacist   pharmacologically
c. association   associative   associate
d. biology   biological   biologist
e. conclusion   conclusive   conclude
f. technology   technological   technologist

  Listen to check your predictions.

 Work with a partner. Take turns pronouncing these word families, focusing on changing stress.

Speak Out

 Giving an Impromptu Talk From time to time, we are asked to speak to a group when we have had little or no time to prepare. For example, at a gathering, you might be asked to tell a story or to give your point of view on a topic. This is called *impromptu speaking*.

When preparing for an impromptu talk, there are a few things to consider.

- Don't panic. Your audience probably knows that you have not had time to prepare much. A few pertinent ideas, presented in a relaxed and confident manner, will go a long way.

- Organize your thoughts as much as possible.

- Be sure to include an introduction with an attention-getting opener and a conclusion with a memorable ending.

- Delivery—eye contact, pacing, volume, a sense of confidence—is perhaps more important in an impromptu talk than in a prepared talk.

In a small group, take turns giving an impromptu talk. A group member will give you a topic from the list. Take one minute to organize your ideas and prepare your opening and conclusion. Then deliver your talk.

- the funniest person you've ever met
- when humor hurts
- what we can do to improve our community
- a job that will be important in the next ten years
- the importance of knowing more than one language
- your opinion on (choose a current topic)

READING and WRITING

Read About It

 Before You Read As a child, did you or someone you know have problems pronouncing particular sounds? How did others react to this problem? How was the pronunciation problem resolved?

 Recognizing Humor Humor is not always easy to recognize, especially humor from a different culture and/or language. Humor often depends on things that "don't fit," which means that you need to know what *does* fit in order to appreciate the humor. It can also depend on wordplay—the manipulation of the sounds and meanings of words. When reading for personal interpretation, an effective reader looks for incongruities, absurdities, and wordplay in order to gauge the effectiveness of humor.

 Read the selection on the next page. As you read, pay attention to absurdities, incongruities, and wordplay. Choose the line or lines that you think are the most humorous. Discuss with a partner.

Speech Therapy
by David Sedaris

Miss Samson instructed me, when forming an *s*, to position the tip of my tongue against the rear of my top teeth, right up against the gum line. The effect
5 produced a sound not unlike that of a tire releasing air. It was awkward and strange-sounding, and elicited much more attention than the original lisp. I failed to see the hissy *s* as a solution
10 to the problem and continued to talk normally, at least at home, where my lazy tongue fell upon equally lazy ears. At school, where every teacher was a potential spy, I tried to avoid an *s*
15 sound whenever possible. "Yes," became "correct," or a military "affirmative." "Please," became "with your kind permission," and questions were pleaded rather than asked. After a few
20 weeks of what she called "endless pestering" and what I called "repeated badgering," my mother bought me a pocket thesaurus, which provided me with *s*-free alternatives to just about
25 everything. I consulted the book both at home in my room and at the daily learning academy other people called our school. Agent Samson was not amused when I began referring to her
30 as an articulation coach, but the majority of my teachers were delighted. "What a nice vocabulary," they said. "My goodness, such big words!"

Plurals presented a considerable
35 problem, but I worked around them as best I could; "rivers," for example, became either "a river or two" or "many a river." Possessives were a similar headache, and it was easier to say
40 nothing than to announce that the left-hand and the right-hand glove of Janet had fallen to the floor. After all the compliments I had received on my improved vocabulary, it seemed prudent
45 to lie low and keep my mouth shut. I didn't want anyone thinking I was trying to be a pet of the teacher.

When I first began my speech therapy, I worried that the Agent
50 Samson plan might work for everyone but me, that the other boys might strengthen their lazy tongues, turn their lives around, and leave me stranded. Luckily my fears were never realized.
55 Despite the woman's best efforts, no one seemed to make any significant improvement. The only difference was that we were all a little quieter.

Our last meeting was held the day
60 before school let out for Christmas. "I thought that this afternoon we might let loose and have a party, you and I. How does that sound?" She reached into her desk drawer and withdrew a festive
65 tin of cookies. "Here, have one. I made them myself from scratch and, boy, was it a mess! Do you ever make cookies?"

I lied, saying that no, I never had.

"Well, it's hard work," she said.
70 "Especially if you don't have a mixer." It was unlike Agent Samson to speak so casually, and awkward to sit in the hot little room, pretending to have a normal conversation.

(continued on next page)

75   "So," she said, "what are your plans for the holidays?"

    "Well, I usually remain here and, you know, open a gift from my family."

    "Only one?" she asked.

80   "Maybe eight or ten."

    "Never six or seven?"

    "Rarely."

    "And what do you do on December thirty-first, New Year's Eve?"

85   "On the final day of the year we take down the pine tree in our living room and eat marine life."

    "You're pretty good at avoiding those *s*'s," she said. "I have to hand

90 it to you, you're tougher than most."

    I thought she would continue trying to trip me up, but instead she talked about herself. "I tried my best to work with you and the others, but

95 sometimes a person's best just isn't good enough." She took another cookie and turned it over in her hands. "I really wanted to prove myself and make a difference in people's lives,

100 but it's hard to do your job when you're met with so much resistance. My students don't like me, and I guess that's just the way it is. What can I say? As a speech teacher, I'm a

105 complete failure."

    She moved her hands toward her face, and I worried that she might start to cry. "Hey, look," I said. "I'm thorry."

    "Ha-ha," she said. "I got you." She

110 laughed much more than she needed to and was still at it when she signed the form recommending me for the following year's speech therapy program. "Thorry, indeed. You've got

115 some work ahead of you, mister."

    I related the story to my mother, who got a huge kick out of it. "You've got to admit that you really are a sucker," she said.

120   I agreed but, because none of my speech classes ever made a difference, I still prefer to use the word *chump*. ◼

3 The humor in "Speech Therapy" is partly due to Sedaris' avoidance of the /s/ and /z/ sounds. How would a speaker more commonly express these phrases? Discuss with a partner.

    a. the left-hand and the right-hand glove of Janet (lines 40–41)

    b. a pet of the teacher (line 47)

    c. the final day of the year (line 85)

    d. marine life (line 87)

4 What impression of Sedaris do you get from this story? Why? Would this story "work" as an example of humor in your culture? Why or why not? If not, how could it be changed to make it work? Share your information with the class.

Vocabulary Check Match the words and expressions on the left with their meanings on the right.

___ 1. hissy (line 9)
___ 2. lie low (line 45)
___ 3. pet (line 47)
___ 4. let loose (line 62)
___ 5. from scratch (line 66)
___ 6. hand it to you (lines 89–90)
___ 7. trip me up (line 92)
___ 8. prove myself (line 98)
___ 9. got you (line 109)
___ 10. got a huge kick out of (line 117)
___ 11. chump (line 122)

a. make me make a mistake
b. made you make a mistake
c. wild animal
d. show competence
e. making a sound like a snake
f. favorite
g. fool; person who believes anything
h. give you credit for doing something
i. not draw attention
j. enjoyed very much
k. relax; not be formal
l. with basic ingredients

Think About It

6 Discuss cartoons, humor columns, jokes, comedy acts, and funny stories that you have seen or heard recently. How do the concepts of incongruity and cruelty apply to your examples? Be specific.

Write: Preparing a List of References

STRATEGY One of the final steps in writing a paper is to prepare a list of references, also called a bibliography. A list of references is an alphabetical list by author of the sources that you used in your paper. Your list gives credit to the people whose words and ideas you incorporated into your paper and allows your readers to find these sources if they want to. When you write a list of references, you must give this information in this order:

Books

1. Author(s) or editor if no author is mentioned
2. Publication date
3. Title of book, italicized
4. Place: publisher

Magazines

1. Author(s) last name, first initial
2. Publication date in parentheses
3. Title of article
4. Name of periodical, italicized
5. Volume, page number(s)

Carter, R. (1998). *Mapping the mind*. Berkeley: University of California Press.

Cerio, G. (2001, August). Artificial sight. *Discover, 22*, 50–54.

Hockenberry, J. (2001, August). The next brainiacs. *Wired, 9*, 94–105.

Silvers, R. B. (Ed.) (1995). *Hidden histories of science*. New York: The New York Review of Books.

Smith, E. E., & Medin, D. L. (1981). *Categories and concepts*. Cambridge, MA.: Harvard University Press.

 Using the guidelines, put the parts of the reference entries in their proper order. Punctuate them and make any other necessary changes. Then arrange the order of the entries themselves as they would appear in a bibliography.

- *Texas Monthly*   January 2002   91 & 155   Willie Nelson Punchline Willie

- *Me Talk Pretty One Day*   David Sedaris   Little, Brown and Company   Boston   2000

- Bill Bryson   *Notes from a Small Island*   1995   Avon Books New York

- *Gene Perret's Funny Business: Speaker's Treasury of Business Humor for all Occasions*   Prentice Hall   Englewood Cliffs, NJ Gene Perret & Linda Perret   1990

Write About It

 Using the model as a guide, create the list of references for your own essay.

  Check Your Writing Exchange completed research papers with a partner. Using the questions on page 38, give feedback on your partner's work. Revise as necessary, and write the final version of your paper.

GRAMMAR

PREVIEW THE TEST Remember to take a few minutes to preview the test before you begin writing. Looking quickly through the entire test before you begin will allow you to plan your time, so you can give added time to the sections of the test that will take longer.

A **Each sentence has four underlined words or phrases. Circle the letter of the word or phrase that is incorrect.**

1. In "I cultures" <u>such</u> traits as initiative, independence, and competition   A Ⓑ C D

                A

<u>is</u> encouraged and valued; <u>however</u>, in "we cultures" cooperation,

B   **C**

group solidarity, and group decision making <u>are stressed</u>.

                                   D

2. Some people <u>believe</u> that "I cultures" are not <u>as</u> favorable <u>to create</u>   A B C D

               A   **B**   **C**

stable friendships and loyalty <u>as</u> "we cultures" are.

                          D

3. Educators <u>believe</u> it is important <u>that</u> the effects of different learning   A B C D

          A   **B**

approaches on <u>students'</u> success rates <u>is</u> studied.

               C   **D**

4. For cooperative learning <u>to work</u> effectively, students <u>must feel</u>   A B C D

                           A   **B**

individual responsibility to the group in order to <u>be able to</u>

                                           C

develop <u>cooperative effective relationships</u>.

                   D

5. <u>Although</u> some students seem <u>to thrive in</u> cooperative learning   A B C D

     A   **B**

environments, other students report that they miss <u>to work</u> on their

                                               C

own <u>because</u> they find working in groups difficult.

        D

B **Complete the following sentences with an appropriate word or phrase.**

By the time students have finished their year (1.)_____ studying abroad, most will (2.) _____ adjusted well to their lives in their host countries. Nonetheless, many of them will (3.)_____ looking forward to their return home for some time, unprepared for the fact that they could find themselves experiencing a different type of culture shock upon their return. (4.) _____ is called reverse culture shock. Some students (5.) _____ start feeling depressed. The depression (6.) _____ caused by the feeling that no one really understands what they experienced in their time abroad. It may seem like people (7.)_____ not really interested in listening to the stories of the (8.) _____ lives overseas. Most students (9.) _____ changed in some ways by the time they return, and these ways may seem strange to people at home.

The stages of reverse culture shock (10.) _____ similar to the culture shock of moving to a foreign country. Initially everything may seem great, but once the first bloom of returning home, seeing family and friends, (11.) _____ familiar favorite places and (12.) _____ favorite foods wears off, a feeling of alienation may take over. For most people, alienation (13.) _____ followed by a gradual readjustment period as the students find ways to incorporate their new perspectives and values into their lives back at home.

VOCABULARY

STRATEGY **MAKE USE OF YOUR STRENGTHS** Answer the questions that are easiest for you first. For example, if your strong point is vocabulary, answering the vocabulary questions first will build your confidence and will ensure that you receive the maximum points for this section. You can then pace yourself to allow time for the questions that are more difficult for you.

A **Find the word or phrase in the box that best completes the passage below.**

cart	out of	over	mileage	down	out
set on	hand	the price	on for hours	low	loose

Unless you've got a lot of time to spare, don't get my Great Aunt Marty talking about her travels because she'll go (1.)_____. She's been just about everywhere, and she loves to tell anyone who will listen all about it. I've seen her take (2.) _____ the conversation at a dinner party after being asked just one simple question. Let her (3.)_____ on a poor unsuspecting party guest who's never met her before, and you won't see that guest again all evening. But, you've got to (4.) _____ it to her. She does have fascinating stories to tell, and most people seem to get a huge kick (5.) _____ them.

Marty is a great storyteller and she is particularly skilled at getting a lot of (6.) _____ out of all her wild adventures. For example, there was the time she found herself in the middle of a political demonstration in Madagascar and was singled (7.) _____ by the police as being a spy. According to her, she had to lie (8.) _____ for a time while the local police were searching for her. Then there was the time she had her heart (9.) _____ surfing the pipeline in Hawaii even though a storm was brewing, and the waves were enormous. Apparently she paid (10.) _____ for that adventure. But to tell the truth, I think she's lucky to have lived to tell that tale at all! Then there's the story about her camping adventures in Alaska. On that trip she decided to (11.) _____ along her poor cat. Can you imagine a cat on a camping trip? Only my Great Aunt Marty would try to do that. Apparently the cat hated it so much that Marty had to break (12.) _____ and go home early. She never tried that again!

STRATEGY

KEY WORD TRANSFORMATIONS Some tests ask students to demonstrate their knowledge of certain words by changing sentences to include them. For this type of question remember, do *not* change the form of the word when you write the new sentence. Check the word order and subject verb agreement carefully after you have written your sentence.

B Choose one of the expressions in the box to write new sentences with the same meanings.

revelation	strive	move up the corporate ladder
trip someone up	prove themselves	get even

1. When working in groups, some people feel they have to show everyone how good they are to gain people's confidence.

   _____

   _____

2. Sam is always trying to get Cody to make mistakes in order to make Sam look better.

   _____

   _____

3. Sam thinks this is how he is going to get a better job.

   _____

   _____

4. But once he gets fired for it, he will suddenly be aware that he made a big mistake.

   _____

   _____

5. In the meantime, lots of his colleagues at work are angry enough to want to seek revenge on him.

   _____

   _____

6. It's important to work hard for success, but Sam would do better to work more cooperatively on his job.

   _____

   _____

WRITING

 STRATEGY

> **ANSWERING ESSAY QUESTIONS** An excellent composition might still earn poor marks if you fail to answer the question or to follow instructions. Read the instructions and the questions very *carefully* and underline key words to make sure that you understand what you have to write about. Choose the question that you have the most to say about. Make a brief outline of your key points before you begin writing. Remember to leave yourself a few minutes to check for and to correct typical mistakes after you have finished.

Write an essay in response to one of the topics below. Allow yourself no more than thirty minutes. Include an introduction and a conclusion.

A. Explain why you think your culture is either more of an "I" culture or a "we" culture.

B. Describe a type of humor that you find particularly funny or particularly not funny. Give reasons.

C. What things do you think students can learn from traveling abroad that they can't learn in a classroom?

PRONUNCIATION SYMBOLS

Vowels

Symbol	Keyword
i	beat, feed
ɪ	bit, did
eɪ	date, paid
e	bet, bed
æ	bat, bad
ɑ	box, odd, father
ɔ	bought, dog
oʊ	boat, road
ʊ	book, good
u	boot, food, student
ʌ	but, mud, mother
ə	banana, among
ɚ	shirt, murder
aɪ	bite, cry, buy, eye
aʊ	about, how
ɔɪ	voice, boy
ɪr	beer
ɛr	bare
ɑr	bar
ɔr	door
ʊr	tour

Consonants

Symbol	Keyword
p	pack, happy
b	back, rubber
t	tie
d	die
k	came, key, quick
g	game, guest
tʃ	church, nature, watch
dʒ	judge, general, major
f	fan, photograph
v	van
θ	thing, breath
ð	then, breathe
s	sip, city, psychology
z	zip, please, goes
ʃ	ship, machine, station, special, discussion
ʒ	measure, vision
h	hot, who
m	men, some
n	sun, know, pneumonia
ŋ	sung, ringing
w	wet, white
l	light, long
r	right, wrong
y	yes, use, music

Irregular Verbs

BASE FORM	SIMPLE PAST	PAST PARTICIPLE	BASE FORM	SIMPLE PAST	PAST PARTICIPLE
arise	arose	arisen	forgo	forwent	forgone
awake	awoke/ awakened	awoke/ awakened	freeze	froze	frozen
			get	got	gotten/got
be	was, were	been	give	gave	given
bear	bore	borne	go	went	gone
beat	beat	beaten/beat	grind	ground	ground
become	became	become	grow	grew	grown
begin	began	begun	hang	hung	hung
bend	bent	bent	have	had	had
bet	bet	bet	hear	heard	heard
bite	bit	bitten	hide	hid	hidden/hid
bleed	bled	bled	hit	hit	hit
blow	blew	blown	hold	held	held
break	broke	broken	hurt	hurt	hurt
bring	brought	brought	keep	kept	kept
broadcast	broadcast/ broadcasted	broadcast/ broadcasted	kneel	knelt/kneeled	knelt/kneeled
			knit	knit/knitted	knit/knitted
build	built	built	know	knew	known
burn	burned/burnt	burned/burnt	lay	laid	laid
burst	burst	burst	lead	led	led
buy	bought	bought	leap	leaped/leapt	leaped/leapt
cast	cast	cast	leave	left	left
catch	caught	caught	lend	lent	lent
choose	chose	chosen	let	let	let
cling	clung	clung	lie (down)	lay	lain
come	came	come	light	lit/lighted	lit/lighted
cost	cost	cost	lose	lost	lost
creep	crept	crept	make	made	made
cut	cut	cut	mean	meant	meant
deal	dealt	dealt	pay	paid	paid
dig	dug	dug	prove	proved	proved/proven
dive	dived/dove	dived	put	put	put
do	did	done	quit	quit/quitted	quit/quitted
draw	drew	drawn	read	read	read
dream	dreamed/ dreamt	dreamed/ dreamt	rid	rid/ridded	rid/ridded
			ride	rode	ridden
drink	drank	drunk	ring	rang	rung
drive	drove	driven	rise	rose	risen
eat	ate	eaten	run	ran	run
fall	fell	fallen	saw	sawed	sawed/sawn
feed	fed	fed	say	said	said
feel	felt	felt	see	saw	seen
fight	fought	fought	seek	sought	sought
find	found	found	sell	sold	sold
fit	fitted/fit	fitted/fit	send	sent	sent
flee	fled	fled	set	set	set
fling	flung	flung	sew	sewed	sewn/sewed
fly	flew	flown	shake	shook	shaken
forbid	forbade/ forbad	forbidden/ forbid	shave	shaved	shaved/shaven
			shear	sheared	sheared/shorn
forget	forgot	forgotten	shine	shone	shone

BASE FORM	SIMPLE PAST	PAST PARTICIPLE	BASE FORM	SIMPLE PAST	PAST PARTICIPLE
shoot	shot	shot	strew	strewed	strewn
show	showed	shown	strike	struck	struck/striken
shrink	shrank/shrunk	shrunk/ shrunken	swear	swore	sworn
			sweep	swept	swept
shut	shut	shut	swell	swelled	swelled/ swollen
sing	sang	sung			
sink	sank	sunk	swim	swam	swum
sit	sat	sat	take	took	taken
slay	slew	slain	teach	taught	taught
sleep	slept	slept	tear	tore	torn
slide	slid	slid	tell	told	told
sneak	sneaked/snuck	sneaked/snuck	think	thought	thought
speak	spoke	spoken	throw	threw	thrown
speed	sped	sped	undergo	underwent	undergone
spend	spent	spent	understand	understood	understood
spill	spilled/spilt	spilled/spilt	upset	upset	upset
spin	spun	spun	wake	woke/waked	waked/woken
spit	spat/spit	spat/spit	wear	wore	worn
split	split	split	weave	wove/weaved	woven/weaved
spread	spread	spread	weep	wept	wept
spring	sprang/sprung	sprung	wet	wet/wetted	wet/wetted
stand	stood	stood	win	won	won
steal	stole	stolen	wind	wound	wound
stick	stuck	stuck	withdraw	withdrew	withdrawn
sting	stung	stung	wring	wrung	wrung
stink	stank	stunk	write	wrote	written

Common Stative Verbs

APPEARANCE	EMOTIONS	MENTAL STATES		PERCEPTION	OTHER
appear	abhor	agree	find	ache	cost
be	admire	amaze	guess	feel	include
concern	adore	amuse	hesitate	hear	lack
indicate	appreciate	annoy	hope	hurt	matter
look	care	assume	imagine	notice	owe
mean	desire	astonish	imply	observe	refuse
parallel	detest	believe	impress	perceive	suffice
represent	dislike	bore	infer	see	
resemble	doubt	care	know	sense	
seem	empathize	consider	mean	smart	
signify	envy	deem	mind	smell	
	fear	deny	presume	taste	
WANTS	hate	disagree	realize		
	hope	disbelieve	recollect	**POSSESSION**	
desire	like	entertain	remember		
need	love	estimate	revere	belong	
prefer	regret	expect	suit	contain	
want	respect	fancy	suppose	have	
wish	sympathize	favor	think	own	
	trust	feel	tire	pertain	
		figure	understand	possess	

Common Verbs Followed by the Gerund (Base Form of Verb + -ing)

abhor	confess	endure	imagine	postpone	resume
acknowledge	consider	enjoy	keep (=continue)	practice	risk
admit	defend	escape	keep on	prevent	shirk
advise	delay	evade	mention	put off	shun
allow	deny	explain	mind (=object to)	recall	suggest
anticipate	detest	fancy	miss	recollect	support
appreciate	discontinue	feel like	necessitate	recommend	tolerate
avoid	discuss	feign	omit	report	understand
be worth	dislike	finish	permit	resent	urge
can't help	dispute	forgive	picture	resist	warrant
celebrate	dread	give up (=stop)			

Common Verbs Followed by the Infinitive (To + Base Form of Verb)

agree	claim	fail	mean (=intend)	remain	tend
appear	come	get	need	request	threaten
arrange	consent	grow (up)	offer	resolve	turn out
ask	dare	guarantee	pay	say	venture
attempt	decide	hesitate	prepare	seek	volunteer
beg	demand	hope	pretend	seem	wait
can/can't afford	deserve	hurry	profess	shudder	want
can/can't wait	determine	incline	promise	strive	wish
care	elect	learn	prove	struggle	would like
chance	endeavor	manage	refuse	swear	yearn
choose	expect				

Common Verbs Followed by the Gerund or Infinitive

attempt	can't bear	continue	like	prefer	regret
begin	can't stand	hate	love	propose	start

Common Verbs Followed by the Gerund or the Infinitive with a Change in Meaning

forget	go on	quit	remember	stop	try

Common Verbs Followed by the Object + Infinitive

advise	choose*	expect*	hire	order	persuade	teach
allow	convince	forbid	invite	pay*	remind	tell
ask*	encourage	force	need*	permit	require	urge
cause						

*These verbs can also be followed by the infinitive without an object.

Common Inseparable Phrasal Verbs

advise against	come over	get by (on)	listen in on	run across
apologize for	come through	get even (with)	listen to	run into
approve of	come to	get in	live up to	run out of
back out (of)	come up	get into	look after	run through
bear up	come upon	get off	look at	stand up to
be familiar with	come up with	get on	look back on	stick to
believe in	complain about	get out of	look down on	stoop to
brush up (on)	count on	get over	look for	succeed in
carry on (with)	cut down on	get rid of	look forward to	take after
catch up (on)	deal with	get through	look like	take care of
choose between/	do without	get through to	look out for	talk about
among	dream about/of	get through with	look up to	think about
come about	feel like	get to know	make up	try out for
come across	fill in for	get up (=rise)	(=become	turn into
come along	follow up on	give up on	friendly again)	turn out for
come apart	get about	go back on	make up for	turn up (=appear
come around	get after	go in for	miss out (on)	suddenly)
come between	get ahead	go through	object to	wait for
come by	get along (with)	hurry up to	part with	walk out on
come down with	get around	insist on	plan on	watch out for
come in	get away with	keep up with	put up with	wonder about
come into	get back	laugh at	rely on	work up to
come off	get behind	let up	resort to	write about
come out				

Common Separable Phrasal Verbs

bring about	figure out	make up one's mind	take away
bring along	fill out	(=decide)	take back
bring around	fill up	mix up	take off (=remove)
bring in	find out	pay back	take on
bring on	get across	pick up	take over
bring over	give away	put across	take up
bring through	give back	put away	think over
bring up	give up	put off	try on
call off	hand out	put on	try out
call up	have on	put out	turn down
clear up	hold up	run by/past	turn off
cut off	look over	set aside	turn on
cut up	look up	show off	turn up (=increase
do over	make up (=invent)	stir up	the volume)
drop off			

WORD FORMATION

In English there are prefixes and suffixes that can be added to a word to change its meaning or its part of speech. Some common ones are shown here, with examples of how they are used to form words.

Verb Formation

The endings **-ize** and **-ify** can be added to many nouns and adjectives to form verbs, like this:

legal		legalize
modern	**-ize**	modernize
popular		popularize
scandal		scandalize

Elvis Presley helped to make rock 'n' roll more **popular**. *He* **popularized** *rock 'n' roll.*

beauty		beautify
pure	**-ify**	purify
simple		simplify
solid		solidify

These tablets make the water **pure**. *They* **purify** *the water.*

Adverb Formation

The ending **-ly** can be added to most adjectives to form adverbs, like this:

easy		easily
main	**-ly**	mainly
quick		quickly
stupid		stupidly

His behavior was **stupid**. *He behaved* **stupidly**.

Noun Formation

The endings **-er**, **-ment**, and **-ation** can be added to many verbs to form nouns, like this:

drive		driver
fasten	**-er**	fastener
open		opener
teach		teacher

John **drives** *a bus. He is a bus* **driver**.

amaze		amazement
develop	**-ment**	development
pay		payment
retire		retirement

Children **develop** *very quickly. Their* **development** *is very quick.*

admire		admiration
associate	**-ation**	association
examine		examination
organize		organization

The doctor **examined** *me carefully. She gave me a careful* **examination**.

The endings **-ty**, **-ity**, and **-ness** can be added to many adjectives to form nouns, like this:

cruel		cruelty
odd	**-ty**	oddity
pure	**-ity**	purity
stupid		stupidity

Don't be so **cruel**. *I hate* **cruelty**.

dark		darkness
deaf	**-ness**	deafness
happy		happiness
kind		kindness

It was very **dark**. *The* **darkness** *made it impossible to see.*

Adjective Formation

The endings **-y**, **-ic**, **-ical**, **-ful**, and **-less** can be added to many nouns to form adjectives, like this:

bush		bushy
dirt	**-y**	dirty
hair		hairy
smell		smelly

There was a bad **smell** *in the room. The room was very* **smelly**.

algebra		algebraic
atom	**-ic**	atomic
biology	**-ical**	biological
mythology		mythological

Her work involves research in **biology**. *She does* **biological** *research.*

pain		painful
hope	**-ful**	hopeful

His broken leg caused him a lot of **pain**. *It was very* **painful**.

pain		painless
hope	**-less**	hopeless

The operation didn't cause her any **pain**. *It was* **painless**.